LEAPING
FORWARD

PATRICK J. PHELAN

LEAPING FORWARD

FINDING YOUR

PURPOSE AND JOURNEY

AS AN ENTREPRENEUR

Published by Advantage Books, Charleston, South Carolina.
An imprint of Advantage Media.

ADVANTAGE is a registered trademark, and the Advantage colophon is a trademark of Advantage Media Group, Inc.

Printed in the United States of America.

10 9 8 7 6 5 4 3 2 1

ISBN: 978-1-64225-610-9 (Paperback)
ISBN: 978-1-64225-609-3 (eBook)

Library of Congress Control Number: 2023910156

Cover design by Lance Buckley.
Layout design by Analisa Smith.

This publication is designed to provide accurate and authoritative information in regard to the subject matter covered. It is sold with the understanding that the publisher is not engaged in rendering legal, accounting, or other professional services. If legal advice or other expert assistance is required, the services of a competent professional person should be sought.

Advantage Books is an imprint of Advantage Media Group. Advantage Media helps busy entrepreneurs, CEOs, and leaders write and publish a book to grow their business and become the authority in their field. Advantage authors comprise an exclusive community of industry professionals, idea-makers, and thought leaders. For more information go to **advantagemedia.com**.

To the two most important men in my life.

My dad, who I lost way too early. You taught me how to take business risks, to pivot in life, to work and play hard, and not to take myself too seriously.

My grandpa Hughes. You taught me the importance of family, being humble, having a competitive spirit, living life in a simple way, and how to play the game of golf.

Rest in peace to both of you. There is not a day that goes by that I don't think of each of you. You both made me the man I am today.

CONTENTS

ACKNOWLEDGMENTS

The Cordish Team—Reed, Jake, Topher, Jersey Mike, and Gary. You took a chance on a guy who was still figuring out his way. Fifteen years later we are still building. Thank you for your belief and trust in me.

The Leap Team. Thanks for buying into my vision and taking personal ownership in what we do. Jon, your steadfast approach and keeping to a plan should be bottled for everyone to learn.

Close personal friends. You know who you are. You keep me humble and push me to be better every day. Your relationships mean everything to me.

My EO Tribe. Thank you for your wisdom, newfound perspective, and mindset.

Matt Reeder. We have become friends while building both of our businesses, and it's been a fun journey. Thank you for everything.

Ted and Betty Meyer. I appreciate the support and wisdom you have provided me through the years. It has been powerful knowing that my in-laws understood what the risk of being an entrepreneur was all about.

My immediate family. Mom, Danny, and Ann, thank you for being there and listening when I needed you the most.

Mitzi, Jenna, and Jamie. You have always believed in me and know how difficult the journey has been. I have learned from each of you more than you realize. I love you so much!

PAT'S BASIC BUSINESS PHILOSOPHIES

1. It is what it is.

2. Control what you can control.

3. Bird in the hand early on. Two in the bush when you can risk it, or when the bird keeps pooping in your nest, or you have too many birds.

4. Family is good to come home to, not to partner with in business.

5. Listen to your spouse! They typically have more common sense than you, even if you don't want to admit it.

6. Don't poke the bear. Feed him so he becomes your friend over time.

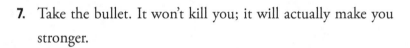

7. Take the bullet. It won't kill you; it will actually make you stronger.

8. Show up + follow through = success.

9. Plan on no plans working out the way you thought they would.

10. Be Gumby while you build.

11. There is no brand until you show you are a brand.

12. Exercise. It's the only thing that will keep you sane.

BONUS FOR A BAKER'S DOZEN!

13. Long term only lasts so long. Pay yourself first.

How I Crossed the Line and How You Can Too

I didn't fit.

And I knew it.

In fact, for years I knew I didn't fit.

Fifteen years ago I was in a cushy job, with a steady, upward climb on the corporate ladder. The pay was great, and the benefits were excellent; in fact, on the surface, it looked like I was on the right path.

But I wasn't.

Corporate America no longer appealed to me, and I wanted to strike out on my own, to start my own business … but how?

I was working for Sprint on a floor full of cubicles. And to most people, I'm sure I was living the good life. However, I'd wake up every morning feeling that I wasn't adding *any* value to the company. I also knew I was made for more, built for more. Deep inside I wanted to own my own business.

At home during the evenings, I spent a lot of time analyzing hundreds of businesses. My wife, Mitzi, always wondered why I would stay up late at night looking at different types of businesses for sale and cranking through spreadsheets. I knew I didn't want to start a business from scratch; I needed to support my family, and I didn't want them to sacrifice because I wanted to leave my well-paying job. After several months I stumbled upon a small company that happened to be in Lenexa, Kansas, called Fast Food Equipment Systems, which was focused on the restaurant industry. After several weeks of studying the company, my background in business development experience told me this was the one!

I was now at the proverbial fork in the road. Do I stay safely behind my desk, hiding in corporate America? Or do I strike out on my own and forge my own path, giving me the freedom and flexibility that I yearned for—and success?

Even though I didn't know anything about the restaurant business, given my MBA in finance and undergrad in marketing, I felt pretty comfortable growing and expanding a business platform. When push came to shove, my decision came down to my personal happiness and wanting to do something that made a difference, something that was my own.

I finally decided to take the "leap" and purchased Fast Food Equipment Systems, with the full support of Mitzi.

Fast-forward to today.

I have owned and grown the Fast Food Equipment Systems, now known as the Leap Companies, successfully for almost two decades. We manufacture cool furniture/case goods; we lead the furniture, fixtures, and equipment (FF&E) logistics for large-scale developments; and through our recruitment company, we help match the best companies in various industries with the most talented people who fit their culture. To date, we have raised more than $100 million in private equity for various hospitality projects, supplied and manufactured more than $75 million in hospitality furniture, and recruited hundreds of talented people for some of the top food and beverage brands. I've also been fortunate enough to be named as one of the Nation's Restaurant News 2018 top 75 power CEOs in high hospitality. As well, the Leap Companies have been named to Kansas City's top 100 growing companies in 2018, 2019, and 2020 by *Ingram's* magazine.

I don't tell you this to brag. As you read this book, you'll find out about the pits I've fallen into, the wrong turns I've made, along with several bad decisions throughout the years. I'm letting you know this because if you are a corporate executive with an entrepreneur's heart, then what you're about to read will resonate with you. You run a division, a segment, or a team within a company you work for and make decisions with an understanding you *directly* affect the growth and expansion of that company. In that respect you have an entrepreneurial mindset. But you no longer feel fulfilled. Now after years of working for that company, you are considering leaving the corporate world and thinking, *What does it take, and do I have what it takes to run my own company?*

Or you may show up physically every day for your job in corporate America, but in your heart you've already left. You're waiting for the right time and the right business to come along so that you can strike out on your own. But you're asking, "What does it take to run a small-to midsize company? Where can I learn valuable business lessons so that I don't repeat common mistakes? What are some of the unknowns I will undoubtedly face, and how do I overcome them?"

You want to be more fulfilled as a person and in business. You're not out to change the world, but you want to provide value and have an impact outside of corporate America. There is an unrest, a churning inside of you that you cannot quiet down. You don't want to be a simple cog in the wheel of business; that's not what *you* are built to do.

Or perhaps you're already an entrepreneur who's growing your own company. You want to know where and how you can learn valuable business lessons. How do you hire the right people? How do you pivot and adapt to the ever-changing business landscape? When does your company need a makeover, and when do *you* need a makeover?

If these and similar questions have been running through your mind, then congratulations on picking up this book!

I've been in your shoes. I've walked your path. I've gone through the inevitable ups and downs of business, and I want to give you the help and understanding you need to make decisions that resonate with you and your business. Using my own business journey and stories from other entrepreneurs, I'll illustrate what it means to own and grow a small- to midsize company. I'll help you understand what the twists and turns look like, what pivoting your business means and what to consider, why you always need to be willing to adapt your business plan to current conditions, and much more!

You're thinking about leaving the nine-to-five world and becoming a business owner. Or you are already an entrepreneur and are looking for guidance to grow your business. I'm here to help you navigate your future so you can have the confidence you need. Whether in your mind or in reality, you're already finding your purpose and journey as an entrepreneur … and I'm here to help you reach your goals!

Here's to your business success!

Pat

CHAPTER 1

The Bigger Purpose That Drives You

Time keeps on slippin', slippin', slippin' into the future ...
—*"FLY LIKE AN EAGLE," STEVE MILLER BAND*

T ick, tick, tick.

When I was in my comfy job at Sprint, I thought I was on my life's career path. I was living what most people call "the good life"—a decent paycheck with excellent benefits. But every day I would wake up hearing the tick-tick-ticking of life passing me by. Yes, I had a solid job, but I was unfulfilled. I was putting in my time, but felt I was stuck in the nine-to-five rut. I yearned for more freedom, more control over what I was doing with my life.

Tick, tick, tick.

Twenty years later I look back at my decision to leave corporate America, knowing it was the best decision of my business life. Don't get me wrong, in the early days of running my own business, I asked myself countless times, "Why did I leave corporate America for this?" But I dismissed the question as quickly as it came into my mind. Why? No matter how tough the road I was traveling, no matter the highs and lows that came my way, I *knew* I was built for this—to be an entrepreneur, just as my grandfather and father had done. As well, my in-laws have continued to run a thriving business for fifty-four years, and they have been great mentors in showing me how to scale a business.

One of the great things about running your own business is that you are creating something unique. You are building a brand within a niche that says, "This is me. This is who I am." Over time you get to revise, rebuild, recreate, pivot, and reinvent your intellectual property that defines your business rather than giving your ideas, your creativity—your life!—to something that would not miss a beat if you were not around.

Kids often grow up saying, "I want to be the next home run champion." "I want to be acting or singing on stage." "I want to hit the game-winning shot." Or some other wild dream fills their minds. Yes, kids have crazy dreams, but most people end up taking a different route and often a more secure path.

But I was created to be an entrepreneur—even though it took me years to figure this out.

When I was a kid in eighth grade, my parents got a divorce. Going from middle school to high school is an awkward time for most kids, but when divorce is thrown into the picture, that time in life can really make you feel lost. But somehow I knew I had to adjust, to evolve, kind of like the TV character MacGyver. I had to adapt to my new circumstances and learn things on my own. And being willing to learn and adjust is a key factor for an entrepreneur. After the divorce, my dad started his own business, and my mom had to go back to work. That meant I had to fend for myself and be my own person. Looking back, I've realized this phase of my life taught me character, independence. I controlled my own fate and learned what I needed to do to survive and thrive. Problem-solving became innate to me. "How do I move forward?" was a question that literally went through my mind on a daily basis. This mindset stayed with me from that point on and is my go-to thinking while running my business today.

Another incident that had a huge impact on my entrepreneurship happened in 1995, soon after I graduated with my business degree from the University of Missouri in Columbia, Missouri, and was getting ready to move into the real world. A few months after the graduation commencement, I got a call from my sister. She told me that my dad was on a business trip and passed away from a heart attack. I remember sitting on my bed feeling like life had thrown me another curveball, and I was feeling hopeless. What should have been an exciting time for me was now "Holy crap! How could I go on without my dad?"

When I got my senses back, I knew I had to pick myself up and move back home to Peoria, Illinois, to help my family. We had to settle the estate and determine what to do with Dad's wholesale insurance business, and I wanted to make sure my younger brother didn't lose his way. Once again this period in my life solidified my need to figure things out and to find the best way to move forward.

During this time Mitzi was my girlfriend and a year behind me in college. I loved her and wanted to marry her, so this was another area of my life that I needed to figure out how to move forward.

While these were tumultuous times in my life, looking back, they taught me how to "pivot" in bad situations and how to not get buried by bad news.

In 2002 I was working for Sprint in what I like to call the "cube farm"—a place full of look-alike cubes—day in and day out. I'm sure that most people would think I was living the "good life," and for the most part, I was! The pay and benefits were great, we had a beautiful home, my wife and kids never lacked anything … but deep inside my soul, I felt empty. I was simply going through the motions at work and not giving my best effort.

Soon after I decided to move on. I went to work for Thyssen-Krupp Access from 2002 to 2006. I rapidly rose through the ranks and was promoted to VP role to direct marketing, merchandising, and business development initiatives to differentiate Thyssen brand from newly acquired Access Industries. My responsibilities grew to the point I managed distribution channels for one thousand dealers, direct stores, and mass merchandisers. I was accountable for new product introduction, collateral development, competitive analysis, industry trends monitoring, pricing, and margins. I was fortunate to increase sales substantially through new product launches.

I was in the thick of the business and enjoyed what I was doing to some extent. But I still wanted to own my own business, as my grandfather and father had done. What could I do that would scratch the proverbial entrepreneurial itch?

If you're in the corporate world and considering leaving the safe and known for the wild and unknown, throughout this book, I want to help you figure out what your path looks like and determine for yourself when the timing is right to make that move. If you've taken that step as a fledgling entrepreneur, I'm sure you feel a sense of elation; you're doing what you're meant to be doing. But there can also be a sense of overwhelm—everything depends on you—and fear and trepidation can set in: What does the future look like? Will I be able to provide for myself? For my family? When and who do I hire? Can I truly grow this company?

I can tell you that all of these thoughts are normal. In fact, they can be a driving force that propels you down the road you need to travel, to get the results you need, and to fulfill your destiny.

THE ROAD LESS TRAVELED

Being an entrepreneur isn't for the faint of heart. If *you* don't grow the company, it will eventually fail. If *you* don't make the sale, you can't provide for yourself or your family. As a twist on the old saying goes, "The buck stops with you." But it isn't fear that drives you. While there are countless people who *want* to start their own businesses, you are part of a minority, albeit a sizable minority in terms of numbers. Consider the following:[1]

- According to the latest entrepreneurship stats, nearly 5.4 million new businesses were registered in 2021 (Census Bureau 2022). Not only is this a 23 percent year-over-year increase, but it is also the highest number of young establishments there's ever been in a single calendar year in more than fifteen years.

---

1   Ying Lin, "10 Entrepreneur Statistics You Need to Know in 2023," Oberlo, January 28, 2023, https://www.oberlo.com/blog/entrepreneur-statistics.

- The latest entrepreneurial statistics show that more than 6 in 10 (78 percent) small businesses in 2020 reported to be profitable (Guidant Financial 2021).

- Figures show that there are up to 4 million firms in the United States that are owned by minorities, and they generate a whopping $700 billion in sales every year.

- The third most popular motivation to start a business is a "dissatisfaction with corporate America." In fact, 25 percent of the current US entrepreneurs say they were driven to entrepreneurship because of this.

- Recent entrepreneur stats show that in 2018, 15.6 percent of the US adult population (aged eighteen to sixty-four) were entrepreneurs.

Now consider this:

- A total of 67.7 percent of the world's richest people are "self-made"![2]

If the above statistics inspire you, then you can be certain that becoming an entrepreneur or growing your already established business is the right path for you. But make no mistake: as a business owner, you'll work harder than you've ever worked, putting in longer hours and making more sacrifices. However, the good news is, if you want to take an afternoon off to go golfing, do some shopping, or simply hang out with your spouse or family, you're the boss, and you don't have to answer to anyone!

Ultimately, you have to decide to bet on yourself instead of someone else. If you are considering leaving your corporate job, ask yourself, "How secure is it anyway?" If the business world tells us

---

2   Lin, "Entrepreneur."

anything, it is that all corporate jobs are one economic downturn away from elimination, demotion, or transfer. You can be let go at any time, so take the time to discover your true potential and purpose.

Whether you are starting your business from scratch or have a viable one, it's easy—and convenient—to look to other people to build a network. However, there will come a point when it is more important that *you* build your business relationships. That's the topic for the next chapter.

PAT'S POINTS TO PONDER

- Whether you are starting your business or own one, it has to be something unique to you, that has your design, your personal identity tied to it.

- If you're in the corporate world and considering starting your own company, do you have a business plan and a road map to follow?

- It is important to have people who believe in you and what you are doing. Who is "in your corner"?

CHAPTER 2

Develop Your Own Business Relationships

Business happens over years and years. Value is measured
in the total upside of a business relationship, not by
how much you squeezed out in any one deal.

—MARK CUBAN

hen I bought my business back in 2005, there were many existing business connections. One manufacturer even told me that I should "stay the course." The problem? These companies didn't know me, and I didn't know them. What we both knew was that the businesses worked well together in the *past* … but would that continue in the future? As the old saying goes, "What have you done for me lately?" So I took the first six months to a year to really get to know my business and business connections. I needed to find out if these business transactions were the right ones for me. Once I had a good understanding of what was working and what wasn't, I put on my let's-grow-this-business hat and started looking outside my current connections to see how I could grow Fast Food Equipment Systems: Where is this company going? How can I branch out into new industries?

In business you can't rest on your laurels, nor should you rely on others or their connections to build your business. And you can't trust that what was good will always be good going forward. This is the lazy man's way of doing business. As an entrepreneur you always have to be moving forward, consistently creating and forging new business relationships. Forging your own connections and relationships will give you a lot more power and leverage to grow your company.

THE TURNING POINT

Here is a truth that you might never have been told: you will never know if you're truly an entrepreneur until you become one. That was true for me.

I remember leaving college and bouncing from job to job but never feeling like I fit in. Because I'm a creator, I get restless if I start to get stagnant. And the eight-to-four or nine-to-five routine of work didn't fit me. I get easily bored and need a constant challenge. I think that's one of the highlight characteristics of an entrepreneur—you always have to "push the envelope," exploring new territory, new ideas, and what-ifs. This is the sweet spot, the comfort zone of an entrepreneur, and it isn't a place of the timid of heart.

Don't get me wrong. I'm not saying there's never any fear or insecurity—there is! But an entrepreneur will see these as mountains to climb and obstacles to go around or over. An entrepreneur will never see these as times to wave the white flag or go and pout in a corner. "Woe is me!" isn't a mantra that enters my mind, and it shouldn't enter yours either. People are depending on us—our families, our employees, and our customers.

A year before I bought my business, I was in my cushy job at Sprint during the day, and at night I was trying to figure out what I wanted to do with my life. It was then I heard a record commencement speech given by Steve Jobs at Stanford in 2005. The following words still resonate with me today:[3]

> Your work is going to fill a large part of your life, and the only way to be truly satisfied is to do what you believe is great work. And the only way to do great work is to love what you do. If you haven't found it yet, keep looking. Don't settle. As with all matters of the heart, you'll know when you find it. And, like any great relationship, it just gets better and better as the years roll on.

As a budding entrepreneur, those words should resound deep in your soul. I'm not telling you to quit your day job—that's a decision only you can make—but I want to remind you that you only have one life to live, and life is short. So ask yourself, "What do I want to do, and how do I want to leave my mark on this earth?"

For instance, when I originally purchased Fast Food Equipment Systems, the company was focused on the manufacturers that we represented and *their* products. I was really just a middleman, and I didn't add a whole lot of value to the supply chain. There were times that I represented twelve to fifteen different manufacturers in a four-state territory, and they would try to dictate my day and what I should be doing. The reps would pull me this way and that, always trying to get

---

3   Stanford News, "'You've Got to Find What You Love,' Jobs Says," June 12, 2005, https://news.stanford.edu/2005/06/14/jobs-061505/.

the most out of my time because they wanted to maximize *their* sales and opportunities, what was in their best interests versus what was in the best interest of my company. I felt like I was thrown back into the exact same trap I was in when working for corporate America; I was working for somebody else and not driving my own plan. I was a true middleman tied to someone else's agenda, not my own. For example, sales directors would fly into Kansas City and would want me to pick them up and take them to their customers. I was simply an avenue for them to get what they wanted. They were always trying to dictate my day and what I should be doing to sell their products to benefit them. As a middleman, manufacturers were always trying to push me into selling more of their products.

I felt trapped. I felt constrained to their ideas and their agenda, and it took a lot of my creativity away. The reason I got into business was to have financial control and personal freedom to do what I wanted to do and when I wanted to do it and to work with the companies I wanted to work with.

At the end of the day, I wasn't building my own brand; I was promoting their brand. It took the better part of the first year of owning my company before I figured out that I needed to evolve the company by developing my *own* business relationships. I was in business not simply to sell a product or service; I needed to have something that added value to the companies I was working with, and that starts with having trusting relationships.

When you get into business, you'll have people telling you what you should or shouldn't be doing, but they are only looking out for their own best interests. That's why you need to develop your own relationships and control the narrative, the agenda. It's okay to be self-serving; if you're always representing someone else, then the other company always has the control and leverage in what you're doing. Every. Single. Day.

As a business person, you should be able to sell any widget because sales are sales, no matter how you slice it. But business is not simply selling a product or service. The reason I'm successful is because I built my own relationships. Sure, people come to me because of the products I sell, but repeat business comes because I have developed trust and rapport. My word is my bond. It doesn't matter if you're selling a service or a product; don't get hung up on what the service or product is—build your own relationships! Relationships first, selling second. Too many entrepreneurs spend so much time trying to make the sale without taking the time to understand their customers and their needs. Being in business is a marathon,

People aren't interested in what you are selling until they are interested in you!

not a race. Running a business is hard because of the financial pressures to stay in the black, pay all the bills, keep food on the table at home, and take care of family needs. But if your customers see you as just another sales guy, then the first time a better deal comes along, you'll be shoved to the side. So don't get so focused on your product or service that you lose sight of the fact that businesses are a reality because of the people who created them. And people aren't interested in what you are selling until they are interested in you!

I have a saying: when you have relationships, you have all the power; no relationship means zero power.

When I realized the manufacturers' reps were taking all of my time, I also realized that Fast Food Equipment Systems had no brand of its own. So I started working on a new business model. I started making cold calls to potential customers throughout the Kansas City area, looking to make my own connections. Once again I wasn't trying to sell anything; I wanted to introduce myself and see how their business was going. I always made these initial calls about the customer, not what I could sell. (By the way, when trying to sell, it's better to say, "I can offer you this or that" rather than say, "I could sell you this or that.") Keep in mind the old adage: it takes one hundred calls to get one potential sale. So don't get impatient and don't give up!

I never gave up. I was determined to evolve my company, and one of the best calls I made was to the Cordish Companies. They were building a large entertainment district in Kansas City called the Power & Light District, which was a huge gamble on their side to redevelop the entire downtown area. Within that district, they had a lot of bars and restaurants. I had the foresight to call the company headquarters, and I received a callback in about two weeks.

A gentleman asked me, "What do you do?"

I told him that I was involved in the restaurant industry and that we do some consulting and wanted to know where he felt they needed help.

He replied, "We are a large developer, and we can get bogged down in the small details. We could use some help managing the furniture and millwork."

It just so happened that two of their main guys were going to be in Kansas City, and the gentleman set up a meeting so that I could hear the details of their project and see where I could help. Now here's the truth: I had no clue what I was doing!

That evening I got out my laptop and designed my first brochure, making it look professional, even though I didn't know what the heck I was really doing. The next day I went to a print shop and had several brochures printed out.

At the meeting they explained in more detail their need for help with furniture and fixtures. In my mind I was thinking that I needed to make a dollar, but more importantly I needed a project to hang my hat on to show what I could do, something to build on for the future. The meeting lasted about an hour, and it went well.

A couple of days later, I received a call, and the gentleman explained that the main guys felt I was a bit too polished—imagine that!—but they were willing to give me a chance. I was given a budget that I could not exceed, and I took the project. When all was said and done, I didn't make a dollar profit. But what I learned and the connection I made were invaluable. From start to finish, I had to figure out each step and what to do, so I was flying by the seat of my pants. But I delivered what was asked, on time and on budget. And the relationship I had developed led to other projects—it was a true win for me! The company saw that I could deliver and responded to their requirements in a timely manner. The redevelopment of the Kansas City downtown district was a project of historic proportions, and I was involved in it. Cordish was our largest customer for several years, and this project led to my company working with other entertainment companies, casinos, and businesses in the hospitality industry.

Sometimes you just have to get involved and let the opportunity take you down its own path. And you will find other opportunities by going down that path.

That one cold call taught me about the furniture and fixture business in hospitality and led to my company securing business with other national and regional brands. All because I wasn't afraid to step out into unknown territory and showed that I could be a trusted partner. Companies didn't care where the booth came from or where the chair came from. They wanted to work with me because they could trust me—that's the bedrock of business relationships!

Things didn't go well for me right off the bat, and they might not for you either. Next, we'll take a look at that.

PAT'S POINTS TO PONDER

- If you want to start a business, don't wait for your dream to make itself a reality. If you're already in business, don't rest on your laurels. Tomorrow waits for no one, and you have to be proactive.

- Every day is a new day, a day to forge your own path and develop your own relationships.

- Developing trust while making sure you're doing the best job possible will lead to repeat business and referrals.

- Don't burn yourself out trying to save a dollar on your business's bottom line. The right investment, whether equipment or employees, will more than pay for itself over the long run.

CHAPTER 3

One Bad Day, Week, or Month Doesn't Define You

> Only those who dare to fail greatly can ever achieve greatly.
>
> —*ROBERT F. KENNEDY*

Life is full of ups and downs, the good and the bad. However, even the worst days can make you a better person—and make your company a better one—if you look past the darkness and realize there are sunny skies on the other side.

I'm starting this chapter on a personal note, one that has had a lasting effect on my family. If you're having a bad day, it can feel like things will never get better. However, the following story will hopefully show you that no matter what you're facing, there is a lesson to learn and a new way forward.

FORE!

When my daughters were young, I wanted to find a way to connect with them and have fun at the same time. Like most kids, they struggled to find their own path from an athletic standpoint, and like most parents, Mitzi and I let them try different sports to see what stuck with them. However, from a team perspective, nothing fit their liking. I've always loved playing golf, so I introduced the sport to both girls together. Jenna, my oldest, was twelve, and Jamie was ten. Both girls readily took to the game, and I could take them to a course individually, or we could play together—it was a win-win! Over the years they have taken private lessons, and both have become pretty proficient.

In high school Jenna and Jamie were on the same team and led their team to the Missouri state championship against eight to ten other teams. They finished in the top six in the state.

When Jenna left for college, Jamie still had two more years of high school. As a junior she was the best player on the team and was chosen as the team's MVP and went back to the state championship as an individual and was in the top forty.

In her senior year, Jamie had high expectations, and having already gone to the state championships, this seemed like a slam dunk. That summer, she had a very successful golf season that led into high school golf that fall. She broke her individual eighteen-hole scoring average, winning several golf tournaments. Going into the high school districts, she was fully prepared.

However, that day, the unexpected happened.

It was a rainy, windy, and cold day, which caught Jamie off guard. The weather got into her head, and she played the worst golf she had played in years. She didn't make the individual state championship, nor did she lead her team to qualify. A lot of tears ensued. She didn't understand how this could happen, and she was completely embarrassed.

But the coolest moment happened the day after.

As a family we were trying to figure out what happened, when Jamie spoke up and said, "What am I going to learn from this?"

I looked at her in surprise, then said, "I think you just learned what you're gonna learn. The fact that you're wondering what you're gonna learn is a lesson by itself." Then I made a statement that fits right in with this chapter. "You've had an incredible year. In fact, you've had an incredible four years as a high school golfer. And one bad day doesn't define you."

Everybody has a bad day. For Jamie, she had the bad day at the worst possible time as a young golfer. That was a big learning lesson for her; she was not going to let one bad day define the rest of her life or who she was. As a senior, she still won the team's MVP and had the best scoring average.

One bad day, week, or month doesn't have to define anyone at any time.

After owning Fast Food Equipment Systems for a full year, I wanted to innovate. I wanted to create a company that was leading the pack. This was it! I was finally in control of my purpose and destiny.

However, business and life have ways to show us that we don't have the control we think we have. At those times we have to learn to pivot, to adapt, to come up with new ways; if we don't, we will succumb to being a victim instead of a victor.

I knew I would change the Fast Food Equipment Systems business model—and eventually rename it to the Leap Companies—but I didn't know I would have to change it so fast. I'm sure you can recall the financial crisis of 2008. Like all companies, we were under a lot of stress: loss of sales, needing to meet payroll, what to do about our overhead and inventory … the list goes on. So I had a choice: wallow in the woe is me and go under or look at the distress we were going through as an opportunity to grow in other areas.

When I started this company, we distributed ice machines and food equipment to food equipment dealers. However, when 2008 hit, with loans to pay and a young family to provide for, I decided not just to maintain my current line of business but also to expand and branch out. It was through this time that I found out I'm pretty good at figuring stuff out.

After doing my research and due diligence, I realized that expanding into the restaurant furniture business was the right fit for my company. That took about two years of a lot of grinding, including sacrificing my salary at times, but I knew I was on the right path, and I loved what I was doing.

I remember talking to some bankers while I was going through the process of obtaining more finances, and they told me that the majority of people would have given up by now. One banker said, "I don't even know why you keep doing what you're doing." Looking back, I realize I had a little blind faith and was probably being naive at times. But the desire to be on my own superseded the things I wanted (e.g., a newer house, a better car), and I knew if I grew my business the right way, the finances would come. And that's exactly what happened over time.

SURVIVING BEFORE THRIVING

Sometimes entrepreneurs get the idea that as long as they are running things, the business is bound to be successful, and their focus becomes, "I envision myself living the good life." They sometimes put their *own* spin on the line from the 1989 Kevin Costner movie *Field of Dreams*: build it and the customers will come.

My position as CEO of the Leap Companies gives me a different perspective on my early years in business. Through the financial crisis of 2008, I felt like I was thrown into the deep end of business and could barely tread water, which is where I learned to survive. And surviving always comes before thriving.

Going through 2008, I had anxiety attacks. I was panicked. We had an SBA (Small Business Association) loan out at the time, which wasn't huge, but it was enough that it would have set us back financially. And I remember sitting at my desk one evening, wondering, *What am I going to do? How am I going to get through this? Do I stay the course? Do I move in a different direction?* But what helped me the most was keeping a positive mindset. Why? Because it's in the pressure cooker of life that you find out just who you are and what you are made of. In my case I was determined to do more than just survive; I was going to thrive. I just had to figure out what the path to thriving looked like.

The lessons learned from 2008 were the same ones that gave me the confidence that my business would successfully navigate the COVID-19 pandemic. I had the assurance that what I was facing would not last, and my business would still be viable and successful. I just needed to find the path through. Nothing in business is permanent: customers come and go, finances are up and down, employees move on to other jobs. The key is not to get caught up in the surprises that come your way, good or bad, but to "ride the wave" and stay on top. By staying on top, you always have a different perspective and can see opportunities, the same ones you couldn't, or wouldn't, see if you felt like you were drowning in your adverse circumstances. My family and I have actually enjoyed some of the time during the COVID-19 pandemic, and quite honestly, we have had a lot of great family time.

THE BIGGER PICTURE

When the pandemic hit, like everyone else, I had no clue about how it would affect my business, especially our sales. As the pandemic started to take over the entire world, I could have easily succumbed to the pervading fear. If our sales tanked, I could lose the business. If my employees left, who would replace them? While I understand these are concerns for all businesses, for me these just meant I had to grind a little harder, become more creative with sales opportunities, and look for avenues to grow my business. For 2023 and beyond, I believe there is going to be a huge renaissance in the hospitality industry. Sure, countless restaurants and even some chains have closed during the pandemic, but either they will reopen or others are going to take their place at some point. I'm in a much calmer place than I was going through the 2008 financial crisis, and that calmness comes from experience. And the great thing about experience is that you can learn from the experiences of others. So let me be blunt: learn from me!

Wherever you are at—creating your business in your mind, taking your first steps, or having an established business—what you are facing will work itself out if you have the focus of mind to think things through and the patience to see things through.

I believe in myself and my team and the direction we are taking. And when we need to pivot, we'll do so. We have enough financial cushion—business consultants will tell you three to six months—to survive the short term if another setback comes. We are not a big company, and we are financially conservative, so we do much of the work ourselves. Financial pressures sometimes push people in the wrong direction, which is why you need some type of cushion and savings to get you through the hard times. Sure, I could hire more staff if I wanted to and be on the golf course every day. But that's not me. I love being in the mix and making the deals. If we hit another slow period of sales, I don't have to hit the panic button. The team that we've assembled all feel that way as well—they all have the entrepreneurial mindset. I think that's really important.

If you want to stay focused on the bigger picture, here are five things to keep in mind:

1. Be prepared.

"Be prepared" is the old Boy Scout motto. Every day you should have a plan for that day and work that plan. But be prepared and flexible enough to know that not everything goes your way. Being prepared is as much mental as it is reality; you need to be prepared mentally so that you're prepared for the reality of inevitable changes.

2. Build your energy.

Nothing will deplete your energy quicker than a long day at the office. Thus, it is important to know what fills you up: exercise, time with family and friends, alone time, a vacation. Revitalizing yourself will clear your head and give you the ability to think creatively.

3. Don't make emotional decisions.

Business can be like riding a roller coaster. When a big sale comes in, you can be on top of the world. But when your best employee goes to another company, you can feel like your business will implode. Emotions are not the same as having intuition. Intuition is the ability to know something without understanding the reasoning. When you are faced with a decision that pulls on your emotions, take a time-out, even if it's only a few minutes. Remember, emotional decisions can compound problems; rational decisions will help you see the way through.

4. Learn from everything.

No matter what you are going through, or have gone through, there is always something to be learned. Don't let fear, especially fear of failure, stop you from learning what you need to so you can move forward. Whatever you failed at today is a building block toward success for tomorrow. I get that in the moment, you may want to chide yourself—or someone else. Failure is not a time to say, "I quit." Failure is simply saying, "That didn't work, but there's another way that will."

5. Move on.

If you've spent any time exercising, you know the next day you will be sore. Your body is going through "growing pains." Every business that is successful went through its own growing pains, and yours will too. Don't get caught up in the loss of a sale or a once-loyal customer taking their business elsewhere. Spend a little time venting your frustration or anger, then say, "Next!" and move on.

Reality tells us all that we are going to have bad days. But destiny asks us we have a choice: feel sorry for ourselves and let the pity party overwhelm us or wake up the next day, get up, put it aside, and keep moving forward.

I'm sure you're wondering what happened to my daughter Jamie. For people with a positive mindset, life comes around pretty quickly, and that's what happened to her. She applied for a prestigious leadership program at the University of Missouri, for which few are interviewed and even fewer are accepted. The day after her bad golfing day, Jamie received an email stating the she had been accepted for the program! To me, that was a wake-up call that her life was transitioning. She went from being a high schooler where golf was her world to moving on with her adult life and creating her new identity.

Jenna also completed the same program, and I couldn't be prouder of both of my girls!

Once you have a vision for your business and some success, it's natural to want to hang on to that vision. But if you do that, you could be holding yourself back. Next, we'll take a look at what it means to "pivot."

PAT'S POINTS TO PONDER

- Big-picture, long-term thinking will carry you through the day-to-day ups and downs.

- How you handle failure and success tells a lot about who you are.

- If you don't schedule times to kick back and relax at times, you will inevitably burn out.

- No matter what happens, you are responsible. How you handle responsibility tells a lot about who you are.

- Solid relationships will help you overcome mistakes.

CHAPTER 4

Pivot! Have a Plan B, C, D, E, and F

A pivot is a change in strategy without a change in vision.

—*ERIC RIES*

I
f you like older comedy shows, you'll love watching the episode of *Friends* in which Ross, Rachel, and Chandler are trying to carry a large couch up a narrow stairway. Ross, in his typical director fashion, yells, "Pivot!" several times as the three friends move the couch up the first set of stairs, then across the short landing to the next set of stairs. After Ross yells, "Pivot!" one more time, Chandler screams, "Stop it!" three times. Ross then meekly replies, "I don't think it's going to pivot anymore," as the friend realizes the couch is now jammed between the inside wall and outside railings. To which Rachel and Chandler respond, "You think!" You can watch the short version on YouTube.[4]

---

4   TheGodAccount, "Friends—Ross Pivot," YouTube, accessed May 20, 2022, https://www.youtube.com/watch?v=n67RYI_0sc0.

Friends … you gotta love that show!

While Ross finally gives up, saying, "I don't think it's going to pivot anymore," the truth is that in business, the ongoing ability to pivot is vital to a company's long-term survival and success.

As an entrepreneurial term, the word "pivot" comes from Eric Ries and Steve Blank's books on what is called the "Lean Startup Movement." With so much uncertainty for entrepreneurs in the business world, the ability of a company to pivot to ever-changing business environments, the needs of clients and consumers, and opportunities for growth and expansion is key for success.

What I've experienced from my own company is that for a business to pivot, its leaders need to be open to shifting to new strategies and not necessarily a wholesale change within the company. For example, there have been times when we've only had to address one particular issue that has been holding us back. The question then becomes, "What new avenues are available for us to overcome this roadblock?"

The Founder Institute has some good examples of pivoting that are a little out of the norm.[5]

- Turning one feature of a product into the product itself, resulting in a simpler, more streamlined offering.

- The opposite of the previous point is also considered a pivot, in which one product is turned into a feature of a larger suite of features as part of another product.

---

5 Founder Institute, "What Pivoting Is, When to Pivot, and How to Pivot Effectively," April 26, 2023, https://fi.co/insight/what-pivoting-is-when-to-pivot-and-how-to-pivot-effectively.

- Focusing on a different set of customers by positioning a company into a new market or vertical.

- Changing a platform, say, from an app to software or vice versa.

- Employing a new revenue model to increase monetization. For example, a company might find that an ad-based revenue model may be more profitable than freemium.

- Using different technology to build a product, often to cut down on manufacturing costs or create a more reliable product.

I can tell you from firsthand experience that it's important for a company to see the need to pivot. For instance, is there a needed shift in business strategy? Have industry demands changed? What about customer needs? All of these affect the bottom line. Pivoting allows you to change your business model without having to reconstruct—or deconstruct—your entire organization or methods of doing business.

WHEN TO PIVOT

A business pivot is the ability to adapt or change from your core product or service. While business decisions will tell you that it's *time* to pivot, business finances will tell you *when* to pivot. After all, you can have great ideas and the right timing, but without the finances in place, your business will stall.

> A business pivot is the ability to adapt or change from your core product or service.

In business, cash flow is king.

When I first purchased Fast Food Equipment Systems, I followed the advice of someone who said, "Once you purchase your company, you're going to run through your cash on hand a little faster than you think. But if you wait until change comes to change your financial model, or try to find new sources of revenue, you'll set yourself up for failure."

I heeded this advice and decided to take out a HELOC, or a home equity line of credit. A HELOC was easier to get than an additional business loan, and it was great to have the security of a line of credit, just in case. And I did, and thank God I did because I had to tap into it whereas the business never would have ever qualified for a loan at the time. The drawback: I felt a lot of extra stress, knowing my family's home was security for the business, but the cash I was able to draw on got me over the initial business "hump." If I didn't have that, my business wouldn't be here today.

When pivoting your company, it can be a delicate balance between what is currently working and what needs to be changed or adjusted to meet new demands. And that balance can be tricky. You might want to consider the following:

1. One part of your business outperforms.

If you have a single feature of your business that outperforms everything else, you may want to consider specializing in that area. It's easy to get distracted, changing one "good" idea after another. But as author Jim Collins says in his book *Good to Great*, "Good is the enemy of great. And that is one of the key reasons why we have so little that becomes great."[6] Becoming focused for efficiency allows you to work smarter, not necessarily harder, giving you the best possible ROI. If you can identify

---

6   Jim Collins, "Quotable Quote," Goodreads, accessed July 19, 2022, https://www.goodreads.com/quotes/701885-good-is-the-enemy-of-great-and-that-is-one.

a single product or service that customers demand, and you enjoy providing, consider pivoting and building around it.

2. The business model isn't working.

There's a saying, "The business of business is business." What that means is that a company is in business to make a profit. But new ideas and motivation can make the business more personal for you as the owner. Yet no matter how personally attached you are to what you are doing, if your company is losing money, then it's time to pivot. In sports this is called "gut-check time." You need to take an honest, objective look at what you're doing and why and do so without emotion or making excuses. What do you need to simply stop doing? What is draining your resources? If needed, don't be afraid to bring in someone who can provide objectivity.

3. You misjudged your customer's needs.

I've been in this position. There was one point in time that we got involved in some actual restaurant operations and partnered with some people to expand a few different restaurant concepts. I thought that one in particular had the makings of being the next "big thing" in the restaurant business, and without digging into the details of how the restaurant would operate and become profitable, I just thought that I liked the meal concepts, the space looked cool and unique, and I wanted to be involved. However, I found out later that combining restaurant concepts with several types of food preparation was a recipe for disaster! There was no way to control the behind-the-scenes costs, including the ingredients, food delivery, and multiple cooking platforms.

The restaurant was designed to appeal to different food palates and a diverse customer base. I didn't fully understand the concept, and at one point I felt like we were simply "throwing food against the wall" to see what stuck. In other words we kept experimenting, hoping that something would gain a universal appeal. As for the restaurant itself, we couldn't decide if we were fast-casual, like Chipotle, or casual dining as per Applebee's. In fact, we realized later that we were creating a hybrid fast-casual, where the customer would "build" their food like an assembly line, and the piping hot cooked food would come out at the end. The menu included pizza, burgers, wraps, salads, and other quick-to-make offerings.

It was a huge menu!

The food was great, but it almost confused the customer. They would look up at the menu, and their eyes would get glossy. We also didn't have a server to help them navigate the menu—and our own staff had a hard time with it.

We opened three of these types of restaurants but could never become profitable. We just took a shot in the dark and just threw a variety of food together without really understanding what we were doing. We had many customers walk in the front door, take a look at the menu, and promptly walk out.

The hard lesson we learned was that having a single, solid restaurant concept and a particular type of food was the best way to grow the business. I also think this is where many businesses fail because they are afraid to define their niche, thinking that if they do, they will lose customers. However, in business school, that's the first lesson they teach you—define exactly what your business is and who the ideal customer is. Don't try to be all things to everyone.

The moment of truth comes when you're ready to launch a new product or service. Sure, what you are offering is exciting to you, but how will the market and your customers respond? As the adage goes, sometimes "the truth hurts." Did you overestimate the need for your product or service? Did the market not respond the way you perceived, even if your initial surveys showed otherwise? Is your price point outside of what your customers are willing to pay? Is your business message simply not clear? Your answer to questions such as these will tell you whether or not it is time to pivot your business. Always remember, pivoting takes cold, hard objectivity.

Keep in mind that not every pivot works, and when it doesn't you can't get down on yourself; you have to figure out how to pivot again. As a small company, you can't always do a lot of market research, and you can't overanalyze. Sometimes you just have to "go after it" and see what works. If something doesn't work, then you need to pivot quickly. I was in this position when I got into the restaurant operations and was trying to grow my company in that direction. But after a lot of time and stress, I realized this wasn't the right direction for me to go in. The good thing: I was moving forward because I was narrowing my focus on what I wanted to do. Always remember that pivoting, whether or not it leads you in the right direction, is always a forward movement because you are further defining the direction you want to go or determining if you need to go in another direction.

If your company is in start-up mode, then you are in a constant pivot mode. You think you know what you know until you *really* know what you know! This means that how much pivoting you need to do depends on the maturity of your company and its products and services. For instance, after ten years in business, any changes within the Leap Companies are either very refined within the context of what is already working, or at some point I may go into something that is unknown to me but is fully aligned with my business philosophy and direction.

However, when I was first growing my company, I was a middleman and was really working for other companies. The margins were low, and I had to deal with the headaches from both sides. So I pivoted. While maintaining my restaurant business, I figured out how to move into furnishings, and when I was ready, I simply walked away from the other manufacturers.

One more thing I'd like to point out. Pivoting is mainly for start-up businesses and happens within the first five years, while the business is figuring itself out. Start-up businesses by default have to be nimble until they reach the place of stability. However, when an established business adds a new service or product, I would call that "adding a new dimension," which is what I did when I added a recruiting services company to the Leap Companies. Knowing where your company is in the maturing process will determine if you need to continue to pivot or if you can take a more long-term approach when adding a product or service.

4. The competition is kicking your butt.

If you don't know by now, the business world is truly dog eat dog. Someone is always looking to undercut your pricing or deliver a better-quality product or service. A word of warning: Never neglect what your competition is doing; you don't want to end up on the outside looking in. If you are consistently being outperformed, then you need to consider how to pivot. Perhaps your industry is overcrowded. Or maybe there's a company that dominates the market. Do you need to take a drastic pivoting approach? Do your business model and sale strategy need a radical overhaul? You'll need to figure out how to differentiate your company from your competition—and do so fast!

5. There is a need to change directions.

When I was ready to expand the Leap Companies by adding on my recruiting company, I was on the lookout to grow my business, and I saw an innovative opportunity in an area that was new to me. It presented the potential to expand into a new industry and increase my company's bottom line. A word of caution: Before committing time, energy, and money for a new product or service, do your due diligence! Then do what feels right to you; go by your gut instinct and trust yourself to make the right decision.

HOW TO PIVOT YOUR BUSINESS

Here's something you'll never hear from successful businesses: there is no playbook that tells you when and how to pivot your business.

While you could use any sport as an analogy for when to pivot, I'll use football. A football team must pivot at different points, before and during the game. First of all, the coach develops a game plan that is unique to the team they are playing. However, when the whistle blows to start the game, pivoting begins. The opposition has different players on the field than was expected. Pivot. The opposition doesn't run its normal play calls. Pivot. One team is behind by halftime. Pivot. Audibles called during the game call for pivoting. An injured player calls for pivoting. The game score in relation to the time left to play calls for pivoting.

In short the philosophy of pivoting can be called "read and react." Just like football, when you are first starting your business, you must pivot—read and react—at various points during the day, week, season, or fiscal year—and do so quickly!—if the business is going to continue to grow.

As an entrepreneur and team leader, you need to be thinking two or three steps ahead, or having contingency plan B, C, D, etc. so you won't have the chaos of flying by the seat of your pants. You should be asking, "What happens if market conditions shift? What happens if customers approve or disapprove of a product or service?" Try to see things from different aspects so that when inevitable changes come, if you are not fully prepared, at least you aren't caught completely off guard.

In 2007 I put the philosophy of pivoting into practice. After doing my due diligence and realizing that I needed to take the Leap Companies into new territory, I knew there were some specific steps I needed to take in order to successfully grow my company.

First of all, pivoting means having a *new vision*. That meant mapping out what my company was doing today and where I could take it in the future. For instance, when I decided to purchase a recruiting company, I first had to ask myself how such a company fit in *and* benefitted what I was currently doing. Not having intimate knowledge or experience in recruiting, I would need to hire the right people while still maintaining a hands-on approach, at least during the initial stages. I also had to answer questions such as the following: How would I grow the recruiting company? What goals did I have? How would I continually innovate and adapt, given there are hundreds of recruiting companies? And most important, what recruiting niche would my new company focus on? Could I take an existing recruiting model and refocus or make tweaks to find a more profitable business model or new service for my customers? What are the new goals I needed to establish?

Next, it is important to *identify areas of growth* that can lead to new business. When I added recruiting as an additional service to our core efficiency, it was a strategic move, not a pivot. I saw the need and expanded our offerings. Adding a recruiting service wasn't out of necessity or change because something wasn't working, which typically is why someone pivots. I wanted to grow our company and saw a cap in what we could do with our core products/services, so I added a service to expand our revenue and potential.

A crucial add-on to the recruiting company was the most robust e-course for recruiting professionals, entrepreneurs, sales-minded individuals, and future millionaires. There was no other recruiting company offering to educate entrepreneurs and C-suite executives, so I knew this would be a solid selling feature and a great way to establish relationships with potential client companies. In the past year alone, our recruiting contracts have doubled.

Finally, you must *continually innovate and adapt*. Think about the automobile industry, for instance. In the industry's early years, automobiles replaced the horse and buggy. Over the next century, companies that innovated and adapted to rapidly changing market conditions and customer demands survived, and those that did not went under. Today we are entering a new phase: the electric car. Will electric vehicles eventually replace combustion engine cars? How will the Big Three—Ford, GM, and Chrysler—pivot to meet their new future?

In the "innovate and adapt" space, companies can be separated into five categories:[7]

1. Precontemplation

In this initial stage, companies are often unaware of their problems or, worse, are in denial. As a general rule, "precontemplators" often wish they never had to change.

2. Contemplation

Contemplators are companies that are aware they face problems and are seriously thinking about what to do in the foreseeable future.

3. Preparation

In preparation for change, company management takes personal responsibility for causing or contributing to the need for change.

4. Action

Companies have reexamined every facet of their business and are taking concrete steps to make necessary changes.

5. Maintenance

After successfully pivoting, company management works to consolidate their gains and prevent relapse while continually reexamining their business and business model to seek out new areas of growth.

---

7   Kelly Graves, "How to Adapt and Survive in an Ever-Changing Business World," Business Journals, April 8, 2016, https://www.bizjournals.com/bizjournals/how-to/growth-strategies/2016/04/how-to-adapt-in-an-ever-changing-business-world.html.

Whether your business is a start-up or established, pivoting is "pivotal" to your growth and success. The willingness to pivot shows that you are adaptable and skilled at making decisions that will benefit everyone in your company and will have a positive impact on your personal life. A successful pivot means you truly understand your business model and the market you are in and will set you up for future successes.

When you're building a business, your focus will be on your business plan and how to grow your company. However, your business's ultimate success or failure will depend on the relationships with your customers and employees. Relationships are built on the human capital of *trust*, and building trust is the focus of the next chapter.

PAT'S POINTS TO PONDER

➡ Think about individuals or teams that you know of that have had to pivot and how they have done so.

➡ Always have a full grasp on your business climate and your company's finances so that you'll know *when* and *how* to pivot.

➡ Consider ways you can build, or increase, your business's rainy-day fund.

➡ Always be adaptable and flexible on a daily basis; your business depends on it.

CHAPTER 5

Build Trust and Own Up to Mistakes ... Even When It Costs You

> Success does not consist in never making mistakes but in never making the same one a second time.
>
> *—GEORGE BERNARD SHAW*

had completed a number of projects for Cordish, the large entertainment company with whom I had established a good trust and business relationship. When they approached me with another project right outside of Busch Stadium, where the St. Louis Cardinals play, it fit well with the Leap Companies.

We were contracted to develop, procure, and install all the furniture, including providing four hundred barstools of a certain type that were to be Cardinal red. So I went to visit the manufacturer to make sure they had the type of stools and the specific "red" I was looking for, and at the end of the day, I left for home feeling confident about the order.

When the truck arrived a few weeks later, I was pleased to see that everything was going according to plan ... until I opened up the back of the truck. When I started taking out the stools, there were some silver ones and some that were red—but not Cardinal red! I now had four hundred barstools that I couldn't use. I thought, *Holy cow! They're gonna fire me. I've screwed up a great business relationship, and they'll never do business with me again.* I felt sick in the pit of my stomach.

Nothing like this had ever happened to me before. After taking a few minutes to gather my thoughts, I called the manufacturer. To make a long story short, they simply said there was nothing they could—or would—do.

Here's the point of this story. Because I had established trust and a good relationship with the entertainment company, they were willing to work with me. Sure, I was accountable and needed to make good on the contract. But they were able to see past the error, and as long as I replaced all the stools with the correct ones, with the correct color, we would all move on. The manufacturer denied any culpability, and getting into a legal fight wouldn't solve anything. Worse for the client, they would be out four hundred barstools. So I never mentioned a word to my client. I simply took responsibility for the wrong order and took the financial hit and replaced all of the stools in the correct Cardinal red from another manufacturer.

Think about this, I went from doom and despair to relief and positive outcome. For a couple of days, I was thinking, *How am I going to survive this?* But instead of getting buried in negativity, I kept moving forward. Mistakes are bound to happen, and how you handle them will determine the survival of your business.

You may wonder what the entertainment company said to me. When I told them I was sent the wrong barstools, I also said, "Don't worry, I'm going to replace them." When the contract was complete, they wrote me a check, and we all moved on.

TRUST IS THE CURRENCY OF BUSINESS

In my opinion trust is the true currency of business. When there is trust, there is relationship. When there is relationship, business transactions take place. As business owners a lack of trust is our biggest expense—with our customers, our employees, and ourselves. It can take weeks or months to establish trust with a customer, but we can lose it in seconds.

WHAT IS TRUST?

Trust is having a "firm belief in the reliability, truth, ability, or strength of someone or something." Trust—or lack thereof—is the result of words and actions. Business strategist David Horsager speaks internationally on the bottom-line impact of trust. He has developed a system with which he teaches leaders how to build the following Eight Pillars of Trust:[8]

- Clarity—People trust the clear and mistrust the ambiguous.

- Compassion—People put faith in those who care beyond themselves.

- Character—People notice those who do what is right over what is easy.

---

8   "The 8 Pillars of Trust," David Horsager, accessed August 15, 2022, https://davidhorsager.com/the-8-pillars-of-trust-the-leading-indicator/.

- Competency—People have confidence in those who stay fresh, relevant, and capable.

- Commitment—People believe in those who stand through adversity.

- Connection—People want to follow, buy from, and be around friends.

- Contribution—People immediately respond to results.

- Consistency—People love to see the little things done consistently.

The trust you have with your team, the trust you place in your vendors, and the trust that you work to earn from your customers will determine the success of your business.

So how do you build trust? That is a question I ask myself every day. One thing I keep in mind is that I cannot take for granted the trust others have in me, and I remind myself *daily* that what I do today will affect what happens tomorrow. Over the years I've found the following points have helped to build trust with those I have relationship, business and personal.

TRUST YOURSELF

The truth is, you cannot conduct business successfully if you're constantly looking to the "experts" on how to run your company. Yes, you need mentors and others to turn to at times, especially when you are first starting out. But at some point, you need to trust yourself. What does that look like?

- You start running any and all advice and guidance through your own filter to see what feels right for you as opposed to relying on outside sources.

- When you mess up or things don't go as planned, you trust yourself to figure out how to get back on track. You learn to separate what "failed" from who you are so you don't get down on yourself.

- You trust your intuition and follow your instincts. When something seems "off," you don't dismiss your intuition and forge blindly ahead.

DEMONSTRATE TRUST TOWARD OTHERS

You may have heard the saying, "To err is human, to forgive, divine." Let's face it: we all make mistakes. And when mistakes and disappointment happen, we can establish trust—and loyalty—by forgiving others and working with them to correct the resulting error. It's easy to cast judgment or jump to conclusions about someone's motivation or competency. Don't set yourself up as "judge and jury"; instead, extend patience and understanding and help everyone involved learn valuable lessons that will be beneficial in the long run.

MUTUALLY BENEFICIAL RELATIONSHIPS

My team and my customers want to know if they have made the right decision to work for or with me. So I've learned to empower my team to take responsibility for their positions and decisions. They also know I won't hold mistakes against them. Each team member knows that I have their back. Doing so gives my team the confidence to take calculated risks and trust their instincts. When it comes to my customers, I make sure that each one clearly understands the value of my products and services, and they inherently know that we do things the right way.

BE TRUTHFUL

I like to sleep at night, and I'm sure you do too. So I've made it a point to be trustworthy and transparent. I don't hide anything from my customers—or my team—and I've been told that I'm too forthright. But I've learned that those I'm in business with can pick up pretty quickly when something is wrong. Even though it has cost me money in the past, I tell the truth about any delays in delivery, and I own up to product defects or a lack of delivery. And that allows me to sleep at night.

I encourage you to be as honest with your team and your customers, just like you want them to be with you. Keep your promises, and when you can't, find a way to make amends. You may lose a team member or a customer now and then because you truly can't deliver on a promise, but you don't want to lose your reputation as a person who is honest and does honest business.

DEAL WITH IT

No matter how hard we try, at any point something can go wrong. But it isn't what goes wrong that destroys a relationship; it is how we deal with concerns and problems that determines the outcome. Always remember that mistakes can be corrected, but making excuses, blaming, and trying to cover up will never be tolerated. When you care about others, they in turn will care about you, and together you can work with any issues.

I can tell you that customer trust develops from the initial contact and continues through service delivery, implementation, and support. At each step, you can either damage or enhance your customer's experience, and the success of their experience is within your control. Be sure to address concerns and complaints fast. Willingly share information. Gain your client's confidence by resolving conflicts as quickly as possible.

THE VALUE OF CONFLICT

While most people see conflict as something to avoid, I see it differently. Handled correctly, conflict can actually build trust and create long-term relationships.

When things don't work out or you have a big challenge with a client and you're trying to get through it together, I have found that when you hold yourself accountable, situations have a way of working out that benefit everyone. And that is always good for business.

When you work through a conflict with a customer— something as small as a missed phone call or as large as a shipping debacle—how you own the situation and your desire to come

Handled correctly, conflict can actually build trust and create long-term relationships.

up with a win-win solution can gain you a customer for life. Why? Because they trust you. They know what they've got in you—a high-valued, trustworthy vendor, someone who doesn't point fingers or shifts the blame but is solution focused.

To state something obvious, when these types of situations happen, once they are solved, they simply go away. But the time in between of feeling anxious and panic, even if it's a small issue, can feel overwhelming. However, I've learned the importance of having *zero base line thinking*[9] and to live by the phrase, "It is what it is" and move on. I don't allow the moment to paralyze me, and I stay proactive. In

---

9   TechTarget, "Zero-based thinking (ZBT) is a decision-making process based on imagining yourself back at the point before particular decisions were made, and free to make those decisions with the knowledge that you have now about their outcome," accessed August 27, 2022, https://www.techtarget.com/whatis/definition/zero-based-thinking-ZBT.

fact, I say this mantra so much Mitzi's brothers have picked up on it, and we drive her nuts with this saying!

I've learned not to get caught up in the "Why did this happen?" or "What went wrong?" type of thinking. When you're in a situation, trying to figure things out will only keep you stuck in the moment. I've found the best way to handle problem or issue is to say, "This is where we are, so let's figure out what we need to move forward and come up with a solution." Figuring what went wrong so we don't repeat the same mistakes is best left until after the customer's needs have been met.

Always remember, it is what it is!

OWN YOUR MISTAKES AND THOSE OF YOUR TEAM

When I get up in the morning, I look in the mirror and remind myself, "The buck stops here." I can confidently say that the "ballpark fiasco" story I opened this chapter with illustrates this. I've learned that owning my mistakes, and those my team makes, is the right thing to do. Doing so tells my customers that I'm accountable and responsible. And I tell my team to never try to cover up something that's gone wrong. We own it together, and we'll figure out what to do together. Maturity tells us that owning up to a mistake is the first step toward a resolution; immaturity tells us to run and hide.

One of my personal core values is honesty. And honesty is akin to integrity. It's easy to point fingers, to blame shift when mistakes are made, and not speaking up, hoping that no one will notice, is even worse. However, if you want to stay in business over the long haul, blame and omission won't get you there. Every decision that is made—whether it works out or not—must be predicated on the type of reputation you are building with your customers and displaying for your team.

When it comes to your team, remind yourself that they are an extension of you. Sooner or later each team member is going to mess up. So figure out ahead of time how you will deal with your team members individually. Each person is unique, and they will respond to you according to their temperament. For example, one team member may only need to hear "Hey, you've made a mistake, so let's figure it out" to feel bad about themselves. Another team member may need to hear "Hey, you made a mistake, so figure out how to correct it and let me know." My point is, you have to know your team and what motivates each person. I like this ancient proverb: "Success has many fathers, but failure is an orphan." Don't make your team members feel like orphans, but set them up for success now and for the future.

When something goes wrong with a product or service they are using, don't go into defensive mode. For example, a customer calls you up and berates you for failing to deliver your product on time. Your initial reaction might be to panic—that's human nature. But consider the following:[10]

> When a person has a reaction to something in their environment, there's a 90 second chemical process that happens in the body; after that, any remaining emotional response is just the person choosing to stay in that emotional loop. Something happens in the external world and chemicals are flushed through your body which puts it on full alert. For those chemicals to totally flush out of the

---

10   Charlotte Johnson, "Did You Know That Most Emotions Last 90 Seconds? Emotions Come and Go; However, Feelings Can Last a Long Time!" CARE Counseling, accessed September 7, 2022, https://care-clinics.com/did-you-know-that-most-emotions-last-90-seconds.

body it takes less than 90 seconds. This means that for 90 seconds you can watch the process happening, you can feel it happening, and then you can watch it go away. After that, if you continue to feel fear, anger, and so on, you need to look at the thoughts that you're thinking that are restimulating the circuitry that is resulting in you having this physiological response over and over again.

A couple of years ago, we were working with a customer to deliver a restaurant furniture package that was a huge deal. It was the customer's second location, and my team was nose to the grindstone on every phase; the delivery date was tantamount to my customer opening his restaurant on time. I had a lot going on at that time, juggling a lot of balls. So what did I do? I wrote down the wrong delivery date on the timeline I keep for all projects on my whiteboard; this was the first time this had ever happened! I'm the guy who is always checking with our customers and vendors to make sure everything is staying on track and on time.

A week before my customer needed his furniture package, he called me up to see if everything was on track.

"Will you have the furniture at my restaurant by next Friday?" he asked.

"Friday, are you sure about that?" I replied. "I've got the delivery date down for two weeks later."

"Nope, it's next Friday."

I went into full panic mode. I didn't play it off, pretending that everything was under control. I admitted my mistake and told him I wasn't sure I could pull this off but to give me a day. I then called two of my major suppliers, and there is where the value of relationships comes in. I told them what had happened, and both agreed to see what they could do on their end. Both called the next morning and said they could meet the revised deadline, and here's why they did so: I have always treated them with trust and respect. They are always paid on time, and I've always communicated clearly with them. My company is a significant part of their business, and I had never put them in any kind of a bind before.

With a great sense of relief, I called my customer and let him know I could meet the Friday deadline! After the furniture was installed, my customer and I shook hands, and he said, "We all make mistakes. I'm glad you owned it and figured out a way to get this done."

No matter what solution you come up with, be sure to contact your customer to let them know what happened and what you are going to do about it. I caution you not to go into a lot of detail, or you run the risk of sounding like you're making excuses. Then offer your solution and ask if it works for your customer. If so, great! If not, see if your customer is willing to work together to come up with what works for them. Finally, when the solution is in place and the problem is resolved, be sure to follow up for your customer's feedback. It's always exemplary or necessary for you to go above and beyond, and a follow-up call or visit can help set things right with your customer and help pave the path for a long-term business relationship.

Pivoting sometimes creates temptations to take shortcuts in business. I know because I've tried it. The next chapter will show you why it's smarter not to.

PAT'S POINTS TO PONDER

- Trust begins with you. Take a good look at the ways in which you are trustworthy and the areas you need to work on.

- Get to truly know your team members so you can learn how to motivate each one individually, and come up with some ways you can build trust and relationships within your team.

- Relay the message to your team that when things go wrong, you will be there to support, guide, and, when necessary, take the issue off their hands.

- Always remember, it is what it is!

CHAPTER 6

There Are No Shortcuts; Everything Takes Time

If you do the work you get the reward. There are no shortcuts in life.

—MICHAEL JORDAN

Six easy steps to grow your business." "Sign up now and learn how to quickly grow your business to six, seven, or eight figures." I'm sure you've heard sales pitches like these or something similar. The great thing about starting a business is the visions of grandeur that we all have. Vision generates excitement, and excitement tell us, "Let's get going!" Excitement can also tempt us into believing the get-rich-quick business schemes that so many people are pitching.

The truth is, business is hard work … hard work each and every day. It's easy to believe the sales pitches you hear because they seem to promise you won't have to work hard—you just have to rake in the money. New entrepreneurs tend to think, *If I just blast the internet with advertising, people will come running to purchase my products and services* or *If I find the right business partner, all my struggles will be over.* The truth is that, in my opinion, about 1 percent of businesses hit a home run the first time they open their doors. That means for 99 percent of us, overnight success in business can take five, ten, or more years. So I caution you against having the "lottery ticket" mentality. For most businesses, it is multiple smaller agreements that keep the business growing and thriving.

Recently, I had a new employee who was hired to focus on my business development say to me, "I've been doing this for six months now, and it simply isn't working." It seemed to me that he was ready to quit.

I chuckled and replied, "Wow, six months! Did you know that I've put in fifteen years in order to get the Leap Companies where it is today?" This employee was actually having some success, and we were paying him a good wage, and he would earn a nice commission once he hit certain goals. I could almost hear him thinking that after six months, he would be selling deals and making placements and would be a gazillionaire. I then told him, "I only started seeing real success five or six years ago, and if you want to give up, that's your prerogative. But anything you do in life that is worth your time and effort is going to take hard work. Get rich quick only happens in movies and sitcoms. So you need to realign your expectations with reality." I went on to tell him he was doing a great job, but there are no shortcuts just because you want to make more money. This particular employee was relatively young, and I had to chuckle at the time at the naivete of youth!

A LESSON LEARNED

Speaking of shortcuts, that's exactly what I tried to do in the early years of building my company.

After I bought Fast Food Equipment Systems, I was really struggling with the business model and trying to figure out how to transform the company into what is now the Leap Companies. I needed to figure out how to pivot the company without putting more money into different initiatives. Instead of working through all of the details myself to determine how I could finance what I had in mind, I decided to take a shortcut and use other people's money. I did this on two different paths, both of which resulted in a train wreck.

In 2010 I decided to make a financial investment to purchase a restaurant from the landlord, as well as work with an investment group with the goal of creating about twenty similar restaurants. I had always liked the concept of building my own restaurant group, and the people whom I had partnered with were willing to license the idea but weren't willing to finance the entire project. I didn't want to double down with more of my own money, so I had to find a way to get there faster, quicker. It was then I had the bright idea of using someone else's money! Someone else would provide the financing, and I would be the managing partner. In other words I was willing to take a shortcut and to take what I felt was the "easy" road to travel. After all, I was going into business to make a lot of money, and if people were willing to help me, all the better!

I was able to find a business partner who was well-off and liked the idea of funding a restaurant group. We initially purchased three more restaurants, and he considered them to be a passive investment. I spent hours going through the model and plan to make each restaurant profitable, including how to pay back my business partner.

I projected X number of dollars in sales for each restaurant, the net profits, and what my take would be. When I finished, I thought this was a no-brainer. The money would be rolling in in no time, and I'd be on easy street!

Sadly, my idea backfired.

There was way more work in running the day to day of multiple restaurants than I could have imagined. I was the boots-on-the-ground guy running around trying to keep these things going, hiring and firing staff, while analyzing how to improve the business model to make the profit that we needed. But no matter what I tried, the best the restaurants did was break even. At the end of the day, if they weren't making money, neither was I. This went on for about two years, with me traveling to different cities, managing these restaurants, and not making a dime. To state the obvious, this was no shortcut!

Worse for me, even though I hadn't put any money into the additional restaurants, I had risked my family's future by personally guaranteeing the leases. This went on for about two years, and I envisioned a financial train wreck in my future. Fortunately, I didn't allow myself to get so caught up in the stress that I couldn't see a way out. I took a deep beath, told myself, "It is what it is," and began to look for a way to pivot out of this mess. At this point, Providence smiled on me.

One day my business partner came to me and said that he realized how hard I was working to make this deal a success. (At the time I was putting in sixty to seventy hours per week, spending countless hours traveling between Omaha and Kansas City, and I wasn't earning a dollar.) He then said, "Pat, how about I take these restaurants and run them under a restaurant division I already have?" Right then we wrote up a separation agreement, and we moved on with a handshake and a smile. He also complimented me on my professionalism and business knowledge, and I said the same to him.

Working out a deal to end my agreement with the other investment group wasn't so easy. Keep in mind this was a brand-new restaurant concept that I helped create, and the investment group consisted of a private investor who was enamored with the restaurant business. On my end I was worried about making enough sales by the end of each week to make payroll on the following Monday.

Then the proverbial bottom fell out in two waves.

First, COVID-19 hit, which closed the restaurants.

The second happened to my business partner. While he was older than me, he was still fairly young, and we got along great. Sadly, on Memorial Day weekend, I got a call from his wife that he had a heart attack and passed away. I was in shock! Soon after, I received another call from his widow, and she said she wanted all of her investment back. I was now doubly shocked!

When I told her that wasn't possible, and we weren't making any money, she didn't care; she just wanted her money. Unfortunately, that's now how the business world works. I explained to her that we all had taken risks, including her late husband. We both hung up without a solution.

I then had a bright idea to sell one of the restaurants. It was in a sought-after, hot area in Kansas City. So I started the process of finding a buyer, and I was surprised there weren't many out there. In fact, the few offers I received were a joke. Worse for me, I had started putting my own money into this particular restaurant just to keep it going. The world was shutting down, and because I was the only one who could legally sign checks, I was fully liable. I remember walking down a street on Marco Island while on a family vacation, going to dinner with my family, and having a panic attack.

Soon after I returned home, I had another call with my late investor's wife, and I told her that, because of COVID-19, we would have to close the restaurant and divvy up the proceeds. But she wasn't willing to listen; she just wanted her money—all of it. I didn't know what to do. She didn't want to take on any of the liability and wasn't willing to work with any changes we came up with. It was obvious the restaurant group could not continue with her as a part of it.

Fortunately for me, a member of the business group I'm part of gave me a great idea: I should buy her out. And if I didn't, there was no way I could do anything except to declare bankruptcy. At first I thought this couldn't work; there was no way I could return her complete investment. However, on my next phone call to the investor's widow, I explained to her that the restaurant was literally worth nothing. After about an hour of back-and-forth haggling, we finally agreed on a buyout. Mind you, it wasn't close to her investment, but she seemed satisfied, something that was important to me.

There are no shortcuts when taking on a business partner, and it is extremely important to be careful when choosing one.

Life sometimes takes fortuitous turns, and soon after I closed the deal with the investor's widow, something serendipitous happened. About a week later, the landlord of the original restaurant I had invested in called me and said someone was interested in buying the space. After a month and several negotiation sessions, I received a check for every penny that I had invested over the past year to keep the restaurant open. And to make the deal even sweeter, I sold the new owner $100,000 in furniture! Sometimes it pays to stick your neck out!

The lesson I learned was there are no shortcuts when taking on a business partner, and it is extremely important to be careful when choosing one. If the business partner is also a financial investor, they are going to want a return in their investment *first* before you make any money. Everyone looks out for themselves; that's simply the way the business world works. Also, the more business partners involved, the more complicated conversations, issues, decision-making, etc. can become.

I tried to pivot my business model and expedite my finances by taking the shortcut of using someone else's money. However, the person making the investment, by default, will have all the power. In my case, in essence I was back working for someone, which is what I didn't want to do when I set out on this business journey. It would have been better for me to go at a slower pace and rely on my own strengths, ingenuity, and financial capital. Instead, I created all sorts of problems for myself. To sum this up, I should have started small, gone slower, and trusted my own business acumen a whole lot more.

It's easy to fall into the trap of thinking you know what your weaknesses are—whether it's financing, knowledge, or a lack of experience—and trying to overcome the gap by bringing on a business partner to make you feel more comfortable. You may think that having a partner will make you stronger, but in my experience this decision only makes things more complicated and actually makes you weaker. It is better to grow as a person and learn and develop yourself versus trying to take a shortcut by relying on someone else, which will only make doing business that much harder. In my case having a business partner set my company back because I'd spent the last three to four years working to perfect my business model. However, if I would have just focused on what I'm doing now, I would probably be further than where I am today. Although we're doing very well as a company today, if I could go back in time, I would reprioritize away from looking for a business partner and focus on growing myself and my business.

While I can't tell you that every bad decision I've made in business has turned out as well as the aforementioned one, what I can tell you is that no matter what happens, I maintain honesty, transparency, and integrity when dealing with people. I also encourage you to do the same. Your personal reputation depends on it, and so does the long-term survival of your business. Here's a good example from my business experience.

THE ICE MACHINE FIASCO

I had owned Fast Food Equipment Systems for about a year, and my company was the distributor for ice machines in our territory. There was a gentleman who wanted to be a subdistributor, and he was going to buy about forty machines at a time, then resell them. He asked for terms, so I told him he could pay me in thirty days.

Unfortunately, 30 days turned into 60, then 120. I thought this guy was going to put me out of business! I had a lot of money tied up in those machines. I thought, *What am I going to do with this debt I'm carrying? Where do I go from here?* The company was going under before I even had a chance to move it in the right direction.

But I had to figure out a way to pull the deal out of the fire. And here's what I did.

After multiple calls that were answered with one lame excuse after another, one morning I showed up at the guy's house with a truck. Needless to say, he was surprised to see me. I asked him, "Where are my ice machines?" and he proceeded to show me them all in an outbuilding. I hit the boiling point pretty quick! A few had been sold, but most were in the building. I let him know then and there I was taking all of the ice machines back to Kansas City with me. And he didn't disagree.

I found out later that I had no legal right to take the machines or even to show up at the guy's house. I should have gone through the proper legal channels, and he could have fought me in court. But when you always do business with honesty and integrity, there are times when you catch a break, as if Providence smiles down on you. This was one of those times for me.

The overall takeaway here is that as a business owner, it is always best to make your own decisions and fund your own ideas. You need to step up and take full ownership and responsibility; don't use others for a shortcut. A guy I know always says, "Do the right thing because it's the right thing to do." That's a great business mantra to live by.

WHY TAKING SHORTCUTS IS BAD FOR BUSINESS

Taking shortcuts means doing something in the easiest, least expensive, or laziest way and, in some incidences, illegally. Here is a stark reality: people who consistently cut corners tend to be morally compromised, low in conscientiousness, self-focused, and impulsive. When a business has a "shortcut" mindset, eventually, customers will realize they're being shortchanged and that the only one winning is the entrepreneur. And they'll look elsewhere. Business loyalty is not something that can be relied on; if a customer has one bad experience, unless you have established a trusting relationship by doing the right thing at all times, they will move on. In fact, a recent survey found that 63 percent of consumers said "it only takes one unsatisfactory shopping experience" to make them stop shopping your brand.[11]

It might sound obvious, but if you do your best to give your customers what they want and need, they will keep coming back. So here is a word of warning: always align what you want—more customers and more sales—with what your customers want—quality products and services, backed by service and guarantees, delivered on time at your best price. Notice I didn't say, "Lowest price." The reason is that people today realize that the lowest price isn't necessarily the best way to purchase a product or service.

We all know that a business is in business to sell a product or service. However, while your customer may want or need what you are offering, they will only buy because of who you are. In other words people buy people *first*, which is why establishing trust and relationships and having honest rapport will build your business as fast as anything else you can do. Think about the simple things such as how you answer a phone, how you make initial contact, and how you keep in contact. Do you take time to find out about your customer's well-being, or are you only about the business transaction?

I encourage you to take some time to review your client relationships and your business processes. Look at these for the long term and critically review whether or not you are doing the right things at the right times in the right places. When you look at newer relationships, make sure you are doing these same things, which will set you up for immediate and long-term success. Ask yourself, "What makes my business the go-to place? What makes my business great, and what makes it successful?" Keep these things at the forefront of all that you do, and you will grow your business at a steady pace.

---

11   Kylee Collings, "Why You Shouldn't Cut Corners to Raise Profits," *Entrepreneur*, March 2, 2022, https://www.entrepreneur.com/article/347019.

In closing, always think about your business in terms of doing things with excellence. When the going gets tough, you may be tempted to cut corners, but it is excellence that will get you through!

If you're a successful entrepreneur, you are used to being in control. Yet there's a time on your career path where you have to take a breath and depend on others. We'll look at that in the next chapter.

PAT'S POINTS TO PONDER

- Think about times when you have taken a shortcut. What were the results?

- Always give your customers the best; they are the ones who keep you in business.

- Take some time to review your client relationships and your business processes. Look at these for the long term and critically review whether or not you are doing the right things at the right times in the right places.

- Do the same as above to prepare for future business.

CHAPTER 7

When You Find a Team Player, Support Them. When You Find an Impact Player, Invest in Them.

None of us is as smart as all of us.

—KEN BLANCHARD

While working at Sprint, we were a team, and I was one of the players. In big business, team players are important; otherwise, the work will never get done. My problem was that I knew I had more to offer, but there was no way to evolve because of the size of the company. Even though I contributed to the overall good of the company by bringing ideas, solutions, and innovative approaches, for the most part, I felt like I was simply a small cog in the wheel of big business. I was hired to do a job, and I was expected to stay within the confines of my job description. While the money and benefits were good, I also felt frustrated. I wanted to move outside of my "box" to be creative, to develop something from scratch, and to make a difference. Looking back, I didn't know it at the time, but what I wanted to be was an impact player, even though I didn't know what that was.

Had I taken a personality profile back then, I would have realized that I am built different. I am wired to be a big-picture thinker. However, coming out of college, I didn't know who I was, and I did what most college grads do: I looked for a good job that paid well. Working for Sprint filled the bill … until I started to get frustrated. It was then that I started my journey of self-discovery.

I feel sorry for those who feel trapped in their jobs but never take the risk to step out and do something different. Fortunately for me, I had a wife who was fully supportive and trusted me enough to let me explore the business world and what I felt I wanted to do in that world. But it also took a risk on my part; I had to be honest and vulnerable with myself and my wife in order to step out.

GROWING YOUR BUSINESS

After taking some time to get my business on a good foundation, I knew that if I wanted my company to grow and evolve, and for the business to grow past me, I had to rely on other people—and you will have too as well. To use a sports analogy, the owner of a team can't be the coach, a support staff, a star player, and a team member. The owner needs to hire others who know what they are doing and are specialists in their roles. In business, successful entrepreneurs have a vision of what their company is, what it does, and where it is going. This is typically defined through having a vision statement.[12]

---

12   CFI Team, "Vision Statement," CFI, updated April 26, 2023, https://corporatefinance-institute.com/resources/knowledge/strategy/vision-statement/.

A vision statement describes what a company desires to achieve in the long-run, generally in a time frame of five to ten years, or sometimes even longer. It depicts a vision of what the company will look like in the future and sets a defined direction for the planning and execution of corporate-level strategies.

The struggle for most entrepreneurs is when to give up control of certain parts of their company. They have created a living, breathing business that reflects who they are and the way they do business. But if the company is going to grow, control in particular areas must be given to others. When that happens depends on how fast and how big you, the entrepreneur, want to grow your company. That could be in year three, five, or fifteen. However, at some point you realize that without the help of others, business will stagnate or even slow down. That is what I call the "tipping point." Do you grow, or do you maintain the status quo?

And if you want to grow, do you outsource parts of your business, like accounting, or do you hire key players? Either way, you have to start trusting others to be responsible and accountable. In my view this is the number one issue for an entrepreneur to tackle once their business model is proven and starts working.

A word of caution. I've known entrepreneurs who were really good at taking a hands-off approach. Their problem was they took both hands off the wheel of their business and ended up in the proverbial business ditch!

TEAM MEMBERS AND IMPACT PLAYERS

To grow your business, you need both team members and impact players. While there is a big difference between these people, both are invaluable. Using a football analogy, impact players are the quarterback, the wide receiver, or the monster defensive tackle. Team players would be the offensive and defensive lines. However, for a team to win games, both types of players are needed.

In business, a team member is someone who is actively involved in the day-to-day operations. This person contributes to the business's overall success by contributing ideas, listening to the ideas that others bring to the table, and working to improve products, processes, and services. They are loyal and respectful and stay in their "lane." They are willing to share responsibility and work together to overcome issues that may arise. Team players are effective contributors, but they need guidance and direction from you in order to do their jobs proficiently. You want to support these people, even on a day-to-day basis, checking in with them, making sure they have what they need to do their jobs successfully. In other words you want to fully support these people. Team players don't come up with new ideas, but they can improve on processes and procedures that are already in play. They put the brand above themselves. When this happens, you can feel confident and comfortable in their abilities. They understand what commitment is all about and will be a solid team member who has the potential to become an impact player.

On the other hand an impact player is a self-starter. They have an entrepreneurial and visionary mindset. These people are the ones who tell you about a problem and their solution to it. And in some cases they tell you about a problem and their solution after the fact because they know your heart and how you operate, and they do business in the same way—kind of like a "mini you." For an impact player, their job isn't just something they do; it's who they are. They want to grow their area or department like a business within a business.

In sports, when the game is on the line, it's the impact players who step up. "Put me in, Coach!" "I'm ready to play, Coach!" These people are unafraid of what is facing them, and they are not daunted by the unknown. In business impact people are the same, and they are the ones you want to invest in.

MAKING AN IMPACT

In my business, Chris, my chief revenue officer and business partner, is a great example of an impact player and someone I continually invest in. When I decided to start a recruiting business, I struck out on the first two people I hired to run this division. Then I interviewed Chris, and he was the person I needed. He was twenty-seven years old at that time and had been a recruiter for another company for about a year. During the interview I could tell he had the entrepreneurial itch—he didn't know it yet. I loved his energy, his enthusiasm, and his buy-in of the vision that I was laying out to grow this side of business. And he wanted the challenge. (That's another big attribute of an impact player; they are up for a challenge and willing to dig in and do what is necessary to get the job done.) As I asked Chris many questions, it was obvious that he saw roadblocks and obstacles as something to overcome, not to succumb to.

Within a year of Chris joining the Leap Companies, we saw about a 300 percent increase in our recruiting placements and commissions. It was obvious that he knew how to sell, so I started giving him more responsibility and encouraged him to come up with his own ideas. So he built processes on his own, and he came to me with ideas on how we could do it differently. He was truly a breath of fresh air! At year two, business increased another hundred percent, and I knew for sure that Chris was wired like me.

Then a problem crossed my mind: What if Chris started thinking, *I could be doing this on my own, with my own company. Why do I need Pat?* It was then I started to invest in him.

First of all I never told him no when he came to me with a new idea. I simply said, "It's your deal, and you can figure out what will and won't work." I made him feel like he had complete control. I supported him in his endeavors, and I invested in some initiatives that he came up with. Some worked and others didn't. But he was growing as an entrepreneur within my business.

Then after a couple of years, I approached Chris with an offer. I called him into my office and said, "I'd like to bring you in as a partner in the Leap Companies. You're doing a great job of growing the recruiting division, so I want you to share in the financial benefits of the entire company." Needless to say, he was happy. But the truth is, if I had not made him a partner, I would have lost him at some point in the near future. He would've said thanks to me, then moved on when a better opportunity came along. As the business grew, I also invested in the infrastructure Chris needed and hired people when he needed them. Now after eight years, the recruiting division is very profitable. Like all good things, it has taken time to grow it, and we haven't taken any shortcuts. The lesson I've learned is this: sometimes you've just got to see it through and ride the ups and downs.

I want to stress that I chose to make Chris a partner after he had proven himself. I knew who he was personally and professionally, and he showed that he could add tremendous value. The point is, don't rush to make someone your partner just because you have a pressing need. Partnering is akin to a business marriage, so you had better know who you are going to the "altar" with.

Whether you are looking for team or impact players, you can't rush their development. But they have to show you they are getting traction—they are moving forward—and they are proving themselves. It's a mistake to promote someone or give them greater responsibility just because you are desperate to fill a position, if they are not ready for it. It's better to outsource for the short term rather than set someone up for failure and yourself for disappointment. There is a gut feel you'll have, knowing what you've got when someone proves themselves by sticking with you through difficult times. And here is a key to look for: when someone puts the brand above themself, it is then you can feel confident that they understand what commitment is all about. They will be a solid team player, and they have the potential to become an impact player.

KNOW THY SELF AND THY TEAM

If you're a one-person business, then you have to be all things to your business—the sales team, the admin team, the recruiting team, and much more. This is called working *in* your business. However, as your business grows, you'll be in positions where you'll have to hire others so that you can do what you do best. This is called working *on* the business.

As an entrepreneur you need to know what you're good at and what you're not. You also need to know what your employees are good at and what they're not. What are your and their strengths and weaknesses? What can be overcome, and what must be accepted for what it is? As a business owner, are you good at hiring, or do you contract out? Are you a numbers guy, or do you have someone overseeing finances? On a personal level, do you focus on big-picture issues, or are you more of a day-to-day person? Do you tend to be easygoing or high-strung? Are your employees good at working together, or do they prefer to work alone? Are they visionary or nose to the grindstone? These types of questions need answered if you and your employees are going to work together at a high level.

GIVING UP CONTROL

Giving up control of any part in your business is one of the hardest things you'll do. After all, who knows your business better than you do? (Hint: There are others who have better skills than you do, so be on the lookout for them.) Control of your business gets you where you want to go in the initial stages, but giving up control in certain areas will move you forward to greater success.

> **Giving up control of any part in your business is one of the hardest things you'll do.**

I recognize that giving up control—any control—of your business can be scary. Anxiety and worry can hound you during the day, and the what-ifs can cause sleepless nights. But if you want your business to grow, then you have to "lean into your fears" by owning them, then push past them. If you allow fear to control your decisions, your company won't grow. The business control freak will get burned out awful quick, and employees will really just be yes people and followers. Always keep the big picture in mind and allow people to grow and develop, taking responsibilities as they step out and step up.

However, you don't want to give up control for the sake of it. You want to do so strategically. For example, for years I have run the day-to-day operations of my business. Then a couple of years ago, I realized I was way past my limit and trying to do too much. So I hired my executive assistant, Andrea, who has been with me for years. And she really knows how to do her job! But I also had to train her on my business and the way it is run. I couldn't simply say, "Andrea, here's your job and job description," then put everything on her desk and leave her to it. Instead, we worked together in the following manner: I did it and she watched. We then did it together. Finally, she did it and I watched. This process took about six months, and now I don't watch her at all; she is so proficient!

Andrea is a great example of why giving up control in certain areas of your business is beneficial in the short and long run. For years I thought about hiring an executive assistant, but one thing always stopped me: hiring this person would cost me money. But as the saying goes, "You have to spend money to make money." My problem was that I focused on the cost of the salary rather than what not having an executive assistant was costing me—in time *and* money.

Andrea is also an MVTP—most valuable team player—and she brings a different energy into the office. She isn't one to say, "Hey, I've got a great idea," on the level that Chris does, but she is someone who likes to "watch over" to make sure things are done right. For example, I had a policies and procedures manual before she was hired—but it was all in my head. After several weeks Andrea came to me and said, "Pat, I think we need to create a manual, and I have some ideas." And you know what? She was right! Her ideas have taken the company to new heights of efficiency. We've worked together for years now, and I can confidently say that I fully trust her.

As an entrepreneur you face the constant paranoia of adding costs that will reduce profits, and having been in this position, I empathize with you. However, when you are stretched so thin that you doing your business—yourself—causes more harm than good, then it's time to figure out what you need to give up control of so you can become more proficient and your business can grow. The support of my business group showed me the need to hire an executive assistant, but I had to find the right person with the right personality. While Andrea had excellent skills and abilities, she didn't know my business, and training her meant I would eventually give control over to her, and I had to prepare myself to do that.

When you hire someone, don't simply dump a load of responsibility on them and expect them to figure it out. You also don't give that person carte blanche to do whatever they choose to do. Earning the responsibility and freedom to make decisions take time, so do this in small steps. I guarantee you there will come a time when you'll say, "They get it," which will give you a comfort level that this person is acting in the best interests of the company and making decisions the way you want them made.

As a side note, Andrea just came back from maternity leave, which meant I had to take over her responsibilities during her absence. I was floored by how much time it took to do her job, and I realized how important she is to the company overall and to me personally. Doing her job made me realize how detailed and how valuable she is. I wasn't able to work on the bigger business picture, and my work with clients was restricted, which meant the business wasn't growing.

As an entrepreneur the most valuable commodity you have is your time. Giving control of particular parts of your business to others frees up your time, making you more efficient and productive. When others can execute without your involvement, your business will become a well-oiled machine: giving up control leads to savings that reduce costs, which pays dividends in all business aspects. You now have extra time to use in a productive manner. You can move faster and work smarter, with greater confidence and clarity.

I get that it can be a struggle to release parts of your "baby," your "bread and butter" to someone else. And I caution you not to do so until you find the right person. Notice I didn't say the "perfect" person; there is no such thing. Also, releasing control comes with trust; you have to trust each other and be willing to work together through the trials and triumphs. You have to know that things are being done the right way, and the other person is doing things the right way. That's what builds trust. And when there is trust, you can let go of control.

ZERO-BASED THINKING

Your business is facing a financial crisis. You're having a struggle creating or revising a vision for your business. You're going through a hiring dilemma. What do you do when you face these types of issues? Stick your head in the ground like the proverbial ostrich? Play lone ranger by figuring things out by yourself and ignoring the input of others?

Entrepreneurs and their employees must always look for a solution to think forward and not get caught up in a current dilemma. There's always a way out! In short it's imperative to have a positive mindset, not one that turns negative whenever a problem or an issue crops up. Popular motivational public speaker and self-development author and guru Brian Tracy understands this well, and he created a concept called "zero-based thinking."

Every problem you face in business is a point of transformation: either your business will grow and move forward, or it will stagnate and eventually go backward. I've been in countless numbers of these transformations, and this is where zero-based thinking comes in.

When your business is in these transformation times, the first thing you need to do is to get crystal clear about exactly what you want, where you want to go, and how you want to get there. Zero-based thinking is an excellent way to think through a decision-making process, as Tracy explains in his book *Goals! How to Get Everything You Want—Faster Than You Ever Thought Possible*:[13]

> When you begin to plan your long-term future, one of the most valuable exercises you can engage in is "zero-based thinking." In zero-based thinking, you ask this question: "Knowing what I now know, is there anything that I am doing today that I wouldn't start again if I had to do it over?" No matter who you are or what you are doing, there are activities and relationships in your life that, knowing what you now know, you wouldn't get involved in.

Zero-based thinking gives you the insightful opportunity to determine if there is anything in your business that you or your employees should do more of, less of, start, or stop. For example, I attended a conference in Washington, DC, and one of the speakers said that if you are struggling with a decision, ask yourself, "What would my 'future' self say about this decision?" Would there be any

---

13   Brian Tracy, *Goals! How to Get Everything You Want—Faster Than You Ever Thought Possible* (Oakland: Berrett-Koehler Publishers, 2003), 86–87.

regret? Will you be able to live with this decision ten years from now? I also ask myself if I can live with the risk I'm about to take. Questions such as these bring a lot of clarity.

GET TO KNOW YOUR PEOPLE

You might be thinking, *What does zero-based thinking have to do with supporting a team player and investing in an impact player?* Brain Tracy sums this up succinctly: "Top people are always open to the possibility and the need for doing something completely different. They are willing to stop doing anything that no longer works. They don't get stuck into a 'comfort zone' and stay there just because it feels good. They are willing to take the risks and the potential failure that goes with embarking on any new course of action."[14]

The question that follows is, How do you find these top people for your particular business?

One of the great ways I've learned to find the right people is by having all potential—and current—employees take a temperament/personality profile assessment, along with other business assessments. I recommend you do the same because it will help you understand who the person is and how they fit into your business. You will learn so much about yourself *and* your team. When you're looking to hire a new employee, it's not just about their résumé and experience; you need to understand if their personality is the right fit for your company's culture.

Chris and Andrea are perfect examples. I needed a true leader and a driver to lead my recruiting division, and Chris is perfectly aligned. In Andrea's position, I need a processor, and she is the ideal person. As

---

14 Thomas Oppong, "Zero-Based Thinking: Principles for Making Better Life Decisions," December 5, 2019, https://thriveglobal.com/stories/zero-based-thinking-principles-making-better-life-decisions-career-growth-wisdom-advice/.

you grow your business, it's imperative that you have the right people on your "bus" and the right people in the right seats. In my business, once I create a position, I always include various personal and business assessments because these give me a great comfort level knowing that this person is fundamentally the right one for the right job.

I've also found that it's better to have people with the right attitude for a particular position as opposed to hiring someone who has the best skill set. Skills can be taught, but attitude is what truly makes a person who they are.

My temperament/personality profiles illustrate that my personal and work ethic drives me to show up every day. I can crank through spreadsheets because I'm a numbers guy. I'm also very proficient at solving problems. When I'm in the middle of working through a difficulty, I ask myself things such as the following: If I'm in the middle of nowhere, how do I get to somewhere? If I've got a problem, why am I limited in seeing the solution? Instead of feeling paralyzed by my circumstances, how can I rise above them? What can I do to fix this? How can I use this to my benefit? And if I don't have a problem to solve or a challenge to overcome, I can lose interest quickly. In the early days of building my business, no matter what came my way, I would think, *Holy cow, I was made for this life! I get to solve problems!*

Entrepreneurship is a lifestyle, and it's important to envision the lifestyle you want to live.

I can't stress enough the importance of understanding your and your employees' personality/temperament. This will help everyone understand how each person thinks and their communication style so that everyone can work together in beneficial ways.

This comes down to the lifestyle you want to live. The truth is that entrepreneurship is a lifestyle, and it's important to envision the lifestyle you want to live. I preach this when I'm onboarding new employees for the Leap Companies. Even though they are employees, I want them to have an entrepreneur's mindset and take "ownership" of their job and responsibilities.

As a potential or established business owner, keep in mind that today's generation isn't interested in a nine-to-five "job" or considering a thirty-year career. What's important to the younger generations is to have purpose-driven work, shared core values, and collaborative teamwork, which all drive business productivity and quality performance.[15]

Over the years I've had to shift when bringing on new employees. Some of this was driven by COVID-19, but much of my "new generation" mindset was in place before the pandemic.

When it comes to the workday, I'm a little old school. I like to go into the office and have separation of space. However, to attract new employees, flexibility is key. Everybody wants personal freedom. Everybody wants a *lifestyle*, not a job. So for several years, we've offered flexible schedules to all our employees. To the best of our ability, we allow employees to have a balance between work and home that fits who they are. For example, we don't track personal time off. We don't set schedules of how many vacation days can be taken. We simply say, "You're an adult, and just like an entrepreneur, you may have to work times that you don't want to work. There are also times that you want to take off for a few days, and we're good with that." As I mentioned earlier, in doing so, we've created an "entrepreneur culture" at our company that works for this generation, which has been one of the main reasons we've been able to hire and keep talented individuals.

---

15   Justin Sachs, "Five Ways Business Leaders Connect Better with Millennial Employees," Forbes, October 27, 2016, https://www.forbes.com/sites/theyec/2016/10/27/five-ways-business-leaders-connect-better-with-millennial-employees/?sh=4994aa1253a2.

WHO TO KEEP AND WHO TO LET GO

As your business grows, one of the toughest decisions you will have to make is regarding your employees: who to keep and who to let go. What makes this decision so hard is that you are dealing with people's livelihoods, which also affects anyone who is dependent on these people.

While I am very much a "people" person—I truly care about my employees—I've also adopted the mindset of one of the twentieth century's most celebrated CEOs, Jack Welch. Welch joined General Electric in 1960 as a junior electrical engineer and rapidly rose through the ranks to become the CEO and executive chairman in 1981, until his retirement in 2001.

Here is a summary of Welch's—and my—philosophy when considering who to keep and who to let go:[16]

- Every company will generally have 20 percent *A* players, 70 percent *B* players, and 10 percent *C* players.

- *A* players are people who are passionate. They have a get-it-done mentality. They are open to new ideas, no matter where they come from, and have a visionary and a what-if mindset. They are self-starters and have the ability to energize all whom they come in contract with. They make business productive *and* fun.

- Those who are *B* players are the core of the company and are crucial to successful operations. A business owner should focus time and energy toward challenging *B* players to grow and develop and to help them figure out how to become an *A*

---

16   Jack Welch, *Jack: What I've Learned Leading a Great Company and Great People* (New York: Warner Books, 2001), 159–162.

player. They may not reach the *A* level, but challenging these people will energize them.

- Finally, *C* players are those who constantly struggle to—or simply can't—get the job done. These people are procrastinators, time wasters, and excuse makers. They can suck the life out of a team or business and can cause resentment or even dissension because others wonder why they are still with the company.

Welch is also very clear about the monetary benefits that each of these types of employees should receive: *A* players should receive raises that are two to three times what is given to the *B* players. *B* players should receive solid increases as recognition for their contributions each year. However, *C* players receive nothing.

There certainly those who feel it's being cruel to cut as much as 10 percent of a business's employees (10 percent was typically the percentage of *C* players cut each year), but as Welch says, it's just the opposite. In my own words, just like a plant or a tree, to keep a company healthy, it has to be pruned from time to time. That doesn't mean you simply "axe" everyone who is underperforming; after all, you hired them in the first place. It's important to find out if these individuals are lacking the support or opportunities needed to do their jobs proficiently. However, there comes a time when you have to say, "Enough is enough!" and let certain people go. For a business to survive and thrive, it takes a culture of candor and openness, and this type of culture starts at the top with you, the business owner.

My mother-in-law, a successful entrepreneur, gave me some great advice when I was starting out. I'll share this with you in the next chapter.

PAT'S POINTS TO PONDER

- If you want your company to grow and evolve, and for the business to grow past you, you'll have to rely on other people.

- Take some time to write out a description of the types of team members and impact players your business needs.

- Identify the areas of your business in which you'll need to give up control, and develop a timeline to do so.

- How you handle problems and issues in your business—with a positive or negative mindset—will go a long way toward the success of your company.

- Every problem you face in business is a point of transformation: either your business will grow and move forward, or it will stagnate and eventually go backward.

CHAPTER 8

The Rearview Mirror Won't Show What's in Front of You

Forget past mistakes. Forget failures.
Forget everything except what you're going to do now and do it.

—*WILLIAM DURANT*

The famous British prime minister Sir Winston Churchill is widely quoted as believing, "The longer you can look back, the farther you can look forward." I can also tell you there are countless business articles written about the importance of looking back in order to determine a future path, and there is validity in doing so. However, in my opinion, there's also a drawback. When driving your business forward, the "rearview mirror" won't show what's in front of you. And if you continually look in the review mirror, you'll end up in a ditch.

We are quickly moving into the post-COVID-19 era. Companies that embrace this new business environment will create their future with new and innovative ways of interacting with their customers. However, business trying to maintain pre-COVID-19 strategies will be here today and gone tomorrow. Forward-planning companies are way ahead of those attempting to return to the past.

In the business world, I see many entrepreneurs who are driving forward while looking in the rearview mirror. The quandary is that these same people "say" they want to embrace the new business climate, but in reality they want to go back to the way things used to be. However, reality tells all of us that we don't have the luxury of living in the past. If you are considering starting or have started a new business, you have to make the decision to move forward and create your own future. The sooner this truth is realized, the better able you'll be to create the conditions for success.

WISE WORDS

One of the best pieces of business advice came from my mother-in-law almost sixteen years ago. Mitzi and I had been married for ten years, and I was seriously considering purchasing Fast Food Equipment Systems. Mitzi's dad and mom have successfully run their family business for over fifty years. Many years ago they decided to leave their very comfortable job to start a music business in what was then the rural town of Kansas City. As the town grew into the thriving city it is today, my in-laws kept their nose to the grindstone and grew their business while raising four kids, three of which now work for the company, including Mitzi.

"Always move forward. Don't look back."

One evening the four of us were discussing my potential business venture. I was ready to jump into the entrepreneurial pool, and I couldn't think of anyone to get better advice from than Ted and Betty. During the conversation my mother-in-law said, "All I can tell you, Pat, is that when you do this, always move forward. Don't look back."

Even today those words continue to inspire me to accept the inevitable trials that are part of business, then to come up with solutions and move on. My in-law's stick-to-itiveness and never-say-die attitude have inspired me, just like I want to inspire you. Remember, it is natural to second-guess yourself when something goes wrong. But those who win in business take the cards that have been dealt and make the best hand possible. As I said in a previous chapter, "It is what it is," and you've got to move on.

THE ROAD LESS TRAVELED

Starting or continuing your own entrepreneurial journey comes with inherent risks. It is a much harder road to travel than working for someone else and enjoying the comfort that a corporate America job brings. And it is certainly the road less traveled.

When I was standing at the fork in the road between my corporate America job and the entrepreneurial path, I had doubts about myself and my abilities, and looking into the future will always contain doubts—it's the great unknown. But the successful entrepreneur will choose to embrace their future, just like their compatriots in the past. To repeat my mother-in-law's words, "When you do this, don't look back." You have one life to live, and you don't want to look back at the end of your years and say, "I wish I had started my own company."

I've been running and growing the Leap Companies for more than sixteen years. Even with the success I've had, once in a while, nagging doubts about the decisions I've made will poke their way into my mind. That's part of being human. But I can't go backward. I can't undo any mistakes. I must continue to move forward, learning from the past so I don't repeat the same errors. This is the most critical mindset to have. Some people say, "I'll dip my toe into owning my own business." Or "I'm going to keep my job and try to start something on the side until it gets enough cash flow, then I may or may not quit my job." In some cases starting a business part-time is the best route; you can go slow and grow. But there will always come a point where you must jump in and learn how to swim. Then reality will tell you that you need to get in or get out—permanently. Otherwise, you will only have a side gig, not a full-time business.

A DREAM YESTERDAY, WILDLY SUCCESSFUL TODAY

Here is a truth: every successful business today started as a dream yesterday.

Here is another truth: the successful businesses of tomorrow will acknowledge the "doubts" of today and find ways to move past them.

Think about the business owners whom you personally know or those in your community. Those who are viable most likely held their companies together with kite string and bubble gum—they did whatever was necessary to keep their business going—at some point. If you are thinking, *What if I start my company and another disaster hits our economy? How will my business survive?* Consider that in the 1900s, there were twenty growth and contraction business cycles, and in the 2000s, we have already had four of these.[17] Each cycle has given companies the opportunity to revise, refocus, and in some cases reinvent themselves, and your business will be no different.

---

17   National Bureau of Economic Research, "US Business Cycle Expansions and Contractions," accessed October 2, 2022, https://www.nber.org/research/data/us-business-cycle-expansions-and-contractions.

You may also think that money is the biggest factor holding you back. But consider the following:[18]

- Coca-Cola was first served in an Atlanta drugstore.

- Kroger began as a bijou grocery store.

- Walgreens began as a single drugstore measuring fifty by twenty feet.

- Nordstrom was founded as a small shoe store.

- Harley-Davidson built its first motorcycle in a backyard shed.

- The Walt Disney Company's first studio was in the garage of Walt Disney's uncle.

Here are examples of companies that started with little or no money:[19]

- Mailchimp, the email newsletter company, is now a $400 million business.

- Lynda, a content library and tech assets company, was acquired by LinkedIn for $1.5 billion.

- Pluralsight, a remote software training business, is now an IPO candidate with a billion-dollar valuation.

Did you know the following facts?[20]

---

18   Love Money, "The Humble Beginnings of the World's Biggest Businesses," accessed October 10, 2022, https://www.lovemoney.com/gallerylist/83820/the-humble-beginnings-of-the-worlds-biggest-businesses.

19   Joseph Flaherty, "50 Big Companies That Started with Little or No Money," HackerNoon, March 20, 2018, https://hackernoon.com/50-big-companies-that-started-with-little-or-no-money-4ef1b68aac25.

20   Vivian Giang, "6 Incredible Companies That Started in a Garage," American Express, June 2, 2014, https://www.americanexpress.com/en-us/business/trends-and-insights/articles/6-incredible-companies-that-started-in-a-garage/.

- Apple began in a small garage in Cupertino, California.

- Hewlett-Packard was started with an investment of $538.

- Amazon's founder, Jeff Bezos, held his first meetings at a Barnes & Noble.

- Google opened for business in a two-thousand-foot Menlo Park garage.

- The Mattel toy company was founded in a Southern California garage.

I can guarantee you that one of the biggest determining factors for all of these companies was the founders had a glass-half-full versus glass-half-empty mentality. You also get to choose which mentality you will have.

GET BACK ON YOUR HORSE

I'm sure you can look back in your life and point to moments that have defined who you are today. Here's a bit of business advice I'd like to pass on to you based on one of my childhood experiences.

I was about ten years old when my mom took me and a group of my friends to horseback riding for the first time. It sure was exciting, and I was full of anticipation from watching cowboy movies. Although this was my first time on a horse, I was sure I would have no problem riding like John Wayne or Kevin Costner.

As we made our way on horseback down the trail following our guide, I thought, *This is easy!*

A couple of minutes later, our guide led us across a shallow creek, and all horses followed dutifully—except for mine. My horse decided it was time to cool off and simply lay down in the middle of the water. This incident makes me laugh today, but back then I was literally freaked out! The guide had to come back and transfer me onto his horse, then coaxed my horse back on to its feet and out of the creek. Back on the trail, I had a decision to make: stay on the back of my guide's horse or get back on my horse. Even though I was scared, I was determined not to let my fear hold me back from riding my horse again. So I got back on, and after a few minutes, I was enjoying myself again.

In business there will be times when you're "enjoying the ride" and other times when the unexpected happens and your company will "lie down in the water"—a contract get canceled, a trusted employee moves to another company, inventory falls short. Once the problem is corrected, you have a decision to make: Do you get back on the horse, or do you decide you're not cut out to be a business owner? While only you can make that decision, I can tell you from experience that, in the long run, it's better to keep riding the horse.

I'll close with this: every company doing business today had to face—and continues to face—an unknown future. The question you need to ask yourself is, "Do I have the mindset and determination to join them in creating a new business landscape for tomorrow?"

When you first establish your company, it will be unique because it represents you. What will keep your company unique is if you continue to be who you are, not who others think you should be. We'll discuss this in detail in the next chapter.

PAT'S POINTS TO PONDER

→ Those who win in business take the cards that have been dealt and make the best of hand possible.

→ Always move forward while learning from the past so you don't repeat the same errors.

→ Acknowledge your "doubts" of today, then find ways to move past them.

→ Don't be paralyzed by the unknown and the what-ifs. Embrace what comes at you!

CHAPTER 9

Be Yourself

You are eager to make the sale. You want to build customer relationships. You know that to grow your business, you have to get out there and make new contacts. You want your business to succeed. I get it. You didn't go into business to fail. But in order to make the sale, to build customer relationships, and to make new contacts, you can't be a chameleon and change to fit what you think others want you to do, and you can't be a "people pleaser." You have to be comfortable in your own skin.

In my business's culture, I tell everyone—including myself—to be yourself means to be genuine. To be genuine means that you aren't perfect, and you accept that others aren't perfect. To be genuine means that you have individual styles, manners of expression, ways of dressing, levels of education and experience, and more. I'm continually reminding people to be genuine, to be authentic. When they are dealing with customers, I don't want my team coming across as robotic, or fake, or even trying to be me. True genuine interaction is what is needed in business, and I want my team to be "real" people when interacting with clients and vendors.

WHEN *NOT* TO BE YOURSELF

"Like it or not, that's just the way I am."

Have you heard someone say this or something similar? Whether you're a solopreneur, or an entrepreneur, or an employee, being yourself does not give anyone the right to be disrespectful toward other people. To illustrate, I'll use a fictitious person (but you might know someone like this).

When it comes to being themselves, Rob has no filter, and Sherry is impulsive. Rob is an astute IT guy, but whatever he feels he says, even if he unabashedly interrupts or controls a conversation. "That guy doesn't know a program from an app," says Rob. "Whenever I'm writing code, everyone needs to leave me alone!" On the other hand, Sherry is a proficient executive, but if someone crosses her … look out! In a packed conference room, she might scream at a subordinate, "That's one of the worst presentations I've ever seen! You should be embarrassed!"

Being yourself doesn't give you the license to express whatever is on your mind whenever you decide to. Being yourself doesn't give you the right to have "verbal diarrhea" anytime your feelings get hurt or an idea you have isn't accepted. Yes, it is important to be authentic and to be true to yourself. But at what expense? The truth is that you can be *too* honest, and when that line gets crossed, other people are bound to get hurt at the expense of your I'm-just-being-honest attitude. Being this way

- could cause you to stagnate because you aren't willing to grow and change. You can lose credibility with others. For example, you are about to meet a new and intimidating client. You tell your team, "I want to win this person's business, but I'm scared, and I need your help." Expressing yourself this way could easily undermine your authority.

- can lead to bad decisions. In this case you are relying on the way you've always acted, behaved. But past experience is not always the best to rely on going forward. For instance, you've always been a person to keep tight control over every part of your business. However, you need to hire someone as a CFO, but you're afraid to give up the day-to-day control of your company's finances, so you can't take the steps to hire the right person.

- is a cryptic way of rationalizing your ineffectiveness. "That's who I am." "That's just my style of leadership." Such statements show your defensiveness, which can hold you back from real growth.

WHEN AND HOW TO BE YOURSELF

To be yourself means that stand out in a way that makes others remember you. But you don't want to be a people pleaser; that's a red flag that everyone will see right away. So how can you be yourself in a world that demands conformity? First and foremost you must understand yourself—your temperament and how you interact with people via your personality, which I'll discuss in a later chapter—and your skills and capabilities so that you know where you can add the most value without overextending yourself. For instance, if you are a detail-oriented person, then you might not be the best person to lead your sales team. If you know how to sell, then you may not be the best person to oversee finances. As an entrepreneur it's vital that you understand where you best fit in your company and what your strengths are so that you can surround yourself with the right people with the skills you need. And when you are looking for the right people, famed business author Jim Collins states, "There are really three parts of this question of the right people. The first is the right people on the bus. Second is the wrong people off the bus. But third is the right people in the right seats."[21]

Be authentic in all aspects of your business and in all your business relationships.

When I first decided to buy Fast Food Equipment Systems, then turn it into the Leap Companies, I was more finance and process oriented. I didn't consider myself a sales-centric individual until I was forced to do it too in order to build a company. But pivoting this way brought out my love to develop business and build relationships. And I was better at it than I thought I was. Now I know that is my core strength in the company. The good news is, I have a good background in finance and accounting, and I can fall into that pretty quickly because I was forced to understand these early on in my career. I'm comfortable understanding that, and I'm also comfortable that other people are experts in areas that I'm not. The key here is to be honest with yourself and vulnerable enough with others so that you don't come across as a know-it-all. Vulnerability and being comfortable being vulnerable are big pieces of this.

---

21   Jim Collins, "Getting the Right People in the Right Seats over Time," accessed October 23, 2022, https://www.jimcollins.com/media_topics/inTheRightSeats.html.

You must also be authentic in all aspects of your business and in all your business relationships. If you're trying to lead a team and you're not yourself and authentic, everyone will see right through any facade you are putting up. For example, when you're authentic, you don't have to have all the answers so others around you can come to you, or fellow team members, and admit when they are having a struggle figuring something out. They will ask for help because they have seen you ask for help.

Another excellent example of this is Mark, my business developer, who works remotely. I hired him during COVID-19 to help build our customer relationships and find new business. The interesting thing about Mark that I didn't know until he felt comfortable telling me was that he does collage art in his spare time. It's pretty fascinating. And I had no clue until he felt comfortable telling me about that, and when he did, he opened up about himself, his passions, and his family life. I also shared about myself, my family, and my love for golf, all of which has created a more open and trusting relationship between us. Although Mark is older than me, there are times when he comes to me with a question or a struggle he is having outside of work. I've learned to put aside my personal biases, judgments, and mindsets and to focus on what he—and anyone else who comes to me—needs at that particular time.

As the front-runner of your company, allowing others to be vulnerable and their authentic selves will make you a better leader and a better person. So I challenge you to set the tone of being yourself around your team, customers, and potential clients. Those under your leadership will invariably follow your path, and your entire company will benefit through the bonds that are created.

I encourage you to get to know your team as *people*, not just as employees, and encourage them to talk about themselves when it makes sense. You will be amazed at how interesting your team members are, what got them to where they are, and what makes them feel comfortable in a working environment. Yes, you will always be looked upon as "the boss." I know that I am. And our employees look at us differently, and it's taken me a while to accept that I'm not included in all the conversations or text threads. But as long as each person feels comfortable enough to come to me with an issue or problem, I'm good with that.

As the leader, here are a couple of ways you can create openness, honesty, and authenticity.

SERVANT LEADER

While you always want people to know that you are the leader, being the leader doesn't mean you always put yourself above others. You may have heard the term "servant leader." A servant leader is someone who[22]

> focuses primarily on the growth and well-being of people and the communities to which they belong. While traditional leadership generally involves the accumulation and exercise of power by one at the "top of the pyramid," servant leadership is different. The servant leader shares power, puts the needs of others first and helps people develop and perform as highly as possible.

If you're going to be a servant leader, then you need to let others know that you are one of the team. Yes, you are the one who's leading

---

22   Robert K. Greenleaf, "The Servant as Leader," Greenleaf Center for Servant Leadership, accessed November 5, 2022, https://www.greenleaf.org/what-is-servant-leadership/.

the vision, the charge, but your team knows that you put your pants on the same way they do.

COACHING LEADERSHIP

Coaching leadership is the go-to leadership terminology in the twenty-first century. While coaching itself isn't new, in business, a coach leader is someone who recognizes and promotes team members' strengths while helping those same team members to understand their weaknesses, with the goal of helping each person improve their skill sets. As defined by Paul Hersey and Kenneth Blanchard in the 1960s, coaching leadership is becoming commonplace in today's business environment because leaders create a positive environment that promotes the development of new skills within the workforce, leading to a confident and competent company culture. Coach leaders are focused on helping their teams and individuals achieve short-term and long-term wins. They build momentum that helps others gain confidence via accomplishing short-term goals that lead to long-term wins. Old-school leaders tend to push their agendas and demand that everyone fall in line. But coach leaders make sure that everyone is aligned on the company's vision and mission statements, then help each team and individual to understand their role and how their personal successes contribute to the company's success. To use an analogy, coach leaders make sure everyone is in the same boat, rowing in the same direction.

LOOKING THE PART

We've taken a look at the "internal" side of what being yourself means. Now let's look at the external.

Part of any company's culture is the dress code. In the twentieth century, business suits for men and women were the norm. In the early part of this century, business casual came into vogue. Now in the post-COVID-19 world, people are used to dressing very comfortably. For instance, the clothing industry has created upscale versions of sweatpants and tops. One company has created a dress shoe version of running shoes. Hairstyles are completely individualized. As expressions of our individuality within our culture in general have changed, businesses have fallen in step.

Chris, my chief revenue officer, is a good example of what it means to look the part. When he joined our company eight years ago, he wore dress shirts with the sleeves rolled down and dress pants. In hindsight he was probably trying to dress the part that I wanted him to play in terms of professionalism. Then one day he came in to work with his sleeves rolled up, and there were his tattoos for everyone to see! I had no idea there were "two" Chrises employed at my company.

I called him into my office and said, "Chris, I hired you because you're a good person and have excellent skills for your job. But if you're not okay with yourself, then how can you expect anyone else to be?"

I had created a dress culture that was pretty casual. We don't have many people dropping by the office, so people are free to wear shorts in the summer and sweat tops in the winter. So I was perplexed about why Chris wasn't himself from the get-go. We had a lengthy conversation, and he literally changed overnight. He began to dress and act in ways that reflected who he was. With customers and potential clients, he showed his own personality, which made him way more effective. In fact, he actually stood out from his competition. He was known as Chris, the guy with the tattoos and hat on backward. And people remember his individualism.

A BALANCING ACT

I understand that when it comes to one's external appearance, there is a balancing act. For example, if a lawyer walked into a court wearing a bandana, sleeveless shirt, and sandals, he would probably lose the respect of the judge and jury. If a suit-and-tie guy marched into a high school classroom as their new teacher, the students would wonder what planet he came from. As a business owner, you have to know your customers and potential clients. Older individuals will be more responsive to someone who is dressed more upscale. Younger people will embrace those who wear casual attire. Therefore, you have to know your audience and how you want to present yourself.

As an entrepreneur you want to set expectations for the dress code during the onboarding process. But ultimately, you want to allow your employees to showcase their individual personalities; ultimately, that needs to be the way they fit into your company. While there is always a getting-to-know-you period at the beginning, if a team member cannot be themselves, at some point they will become resentful and feel unfulfilled and will start looking for a new job. They're not going to feel comfortable being themselves; they will not last as an employee. And if they stay with you because you offer a good salary and benefits, their contributions as a team player will be limited, and they rarely will become an impact player. A dress code is one thing, but the person you hired has a skill set that you need, so let them shine by being the person they are inside because that is the person you need.

WORKING WITH CLIENTS

Everything I've said about allowing your team members to be themselves holds true with you, the business owner. This is even more important when you're with your customers and potential clients. For example, you meet a potential client who tells you about the school he graduated from or the business she has been a part of. The client asks about your experience, and if you don't have a higher ed degree or years of experience, what will you say? How will you show your true self?

I've been in this type of situation.

My company was competing against several others for a client's business. I knew that other companies had more experience and greater reach, so I flew down to the client's headquarters for a meeting. After exchanging pleasantries with the owner, I positioned myself as a small business entrepreneur who started my company from scratch. I then showed my portfolio, giving examples and reasons about why this client should do business with my company. This was my way of showing vulnerability and being true to myself.

I told him about how I've grown the company and why and how I brought on particular staff, then got personal about my likes and dislikes and how I like to do business. As I wrapped up, I let him know that my company was fast growing but was small enough to have deep relationships with our clients.

Then it was his turn.

And I was amazed at how similar his story was to mine. He had started a restaurant from scratch on his own, struggled for many years, kept it alive, and kept his dream alive. His company now oversees fifty restaurants, but he could identify with my company, and that was when an instant bond formed. Bottom line: I was able to secure the business because I wasn't afraid to talk a little bit about my and my team's struggles and imperfections and how we've built the company together. That meeting has built a solid relationship from day one, which has been ultra-important through the years.

REAPING THE BENEFITS

You might be wondering, *What is the importance of helping people be true to themselves to my business? Why is it important to develop authentic relationships?*

The answers are twofold.

First, and most obvious, is that you are creating tighter and trusting relationships internally and externally. You are also creating a tighter bond within your company itself.

Second, it's my opinion that customers and potential clients see through individuals who aren't themselves. These people want to know they aren't simply a transaction, and most people want to get to know you—and vice versa—before doing business. So cultivating relationships is of utmost importance. Don't try to rush into a business relationship. Trust takes time to develop, and customers and potential clients want to know you have their best interests at heart—not just their pocketbook.

From a big-picture perspective, if you're not yourself, then you are not going to enjoy what you're doing. If you're not enjoying what you're doing, then you won't be effective leading your company— these all revolve around everyone in your company being themselves. And if you're not comfortable with who you are in your company, you won't stay there very long because you are still trying to figure out yourself. That's exactly what happened to me.

Throughout my career I continued to change jobs because I was looking for my identity that I knew would bring me internal happiness. I knew I wanted the freedom to create my own path in life, and I didn't have that while working for someone else. I was who whatever company I worked for wanted me to be, but I wasn't being true to myself or being authentic. I was searching, going from job to job, but doing so led me to the path I'm now on, one that fulfills me, even through the inevitable ups and downs of business.

If you're someone who has aspirations of being an entrepreneur, or you just started your business, I'm here to tell you that confidence comes with knowing you were built to be a business owner, and fulfillment comes when you are truly building the business you want to work in. I'll also tell you that if you are not fulfilled, then you are not doing what you are meant to do. At some point you have to jump into the pool. Don't be afraid of the risk; instead, focus on the reward.

As your business grows, you can't do everything by yourself. But how do you find the right people to be in business with? We'll look at that in the next chapter.

LEAPING FORWARD ↑

PAT'S POINTS TO PONDER

- Being yourself through authenticity is the most important business card you can give to someone.

- Being a servant leader and having coaching leadership skills will help you recruit and keep the best talent.

- Allowing people to be themselves will reap their loyalty.

- In every area of your business, don't be afraid of the risk; instead, focus on the reward.

CHAPTER 10

Finding the Right Business Partners (You Can't Do It All Yourself)

Coming together is the beginning. Keeping together is progress. Working together is success.

—HENRY FORD

About ten years ago, I was struggling with my company. As the proverbial "jack-of-all-trades, master of none," I was trying to be all things to my company, and it was wearing me out. As well, my company wasn't focused on one or two strategic areas, like we are today, and if someone asked me exactly what my company provided, I had a hard time articulating precisely what we did.

Back then we were a company of one person … me! So I went to a marketing agency for help. We talked about my company's core strengths and products, and they did a great job of helping me communicate our message in a way that was marketable and brandable. We spent many hours talking through our business model, what we do best, and how we do it. And in my opinion, the marketing company really hit a home run, including building a website and marketing message that gave our customers clarity regarding products and services and how to contact us. Knowing my core business offerings, and how to brand and market my company, gave me a ton of confidence. I was able to see that in the hospitality furnishings and recruiting side of the business. This laid a solid foundation and gave me a business direction, instead of just being in business to make money. This was also the catalyst to knowing how and when to grow my team and who to hire. Today my team and I have a clear understanding of who we are and what we do, which has led us to the success we now have.

Depending on what stage you are in the business, a business partner, such as the marketing firm I hired, can be a real asset. However, you don't want to bring in any partner—you want to bring in the *right* one. Certainly, this person or company has to have the business acumen you are looking for; that is a given. But the right partner is someone who understands you—the way you think, the way you do business, the way you interact with employees and customers. In other words the right partner will understand the "human" side of you, not just your business mindset. A partner is someone who can take over aspects of your business so that you are free to concentrate on areas that you do best. For example, at some point all businesses need a bookkeeper or an accountant. This person needs to understand accounting, state and federal laws, and the like, and this is a position that can be outsourced. In that sense the person or company that is outsourced is a business partner.

I have also brought in a business partner—someone who is outside of our company yet has become integral to the way we do business—who has helped us define and redefine my company's culture, which helps everyone understand the way we do business. This isn't something I could have done myself, so having an expert in this area took a lot of pressure off my shoulders.

Your business takes on a life of its own. It needs constant attention to grow and maintain its health, and you have to make continual investments into your company if you want any level of sustained growth. Just because you've figured something at once doesn't mean you can rest on your laurels. There is a constant need of tweaking, changing, and even starting over when necessary. You also have to know when to give over control of parts of your business to employees or business partners. I can tell you firsthand that this is the healthiest way for you to grow your business. In my case we have gone from one to ten employees, with several outside business partners. I can also tell you that who we thought we were a year ago as a company is not who we are today.

TIME VERSUS MONEY

When to outsource comes down to time versus money. The question to ask is, "If I outsource an area of my business, will doing so save me time and money?" For example, as your business continues to grow and expand, at some point an attorney will be needed. As a rule, attorneys get a bad rap, but I have hired some very reputable people **When to outsource comes down to time versus money.** who have saved me time and money in some sticky situations.

Vendors are another way to outsource. When you team up with a vendor, this company becomes a true partner because there is equity at stake for both of you. Vendors are a third party that you outsource to take over certain business functions to take off your plate.

My earlier reference to a bookkeeper is a prime example.

For many years I was the CFO of my company. I always felt like one of my superpowers is that I really get into problem-solving. Whenever there is a problem, I dig into it until I figure it out, so finances were a natural fit. (I have also been the head of marketing, the head of sales, the head of ... you name it, I wore it.) But there came a time when I needed to release the financial side of my business to someone who was more proficient. I was spending way too much time on this area, so I decided it made more sense to let someone else take over so I could concentrate on growing the overall business. After doing my due diligence, I hired Angie because she understood the "human" side of me and not just how accounting works. She could align with me.

I found Angie through another business project. I was super-impressed with her as a person and her skill sets. I was drowned in accounting, which was taking up a lot of my time, and asked if she could help. I agreed, and she jumped right in and helped build a lot of the accounting processes that we use today that have enabled us to grow and scale and help people work remotely. Angie has had a significant impact on my company, with me still having overall financial control. Our companies have grown together, and her company has exploded too. It's been kind of neat watching both of our companies expand and grow, but without her coming to me at a certain point in time, my company probably wouldn't be where we're at today because she lends a lot of experience that I just don't have. So vendors can be a great answer to the time versus money dilemma.

SIZE AND SCALE

The types of partnership decisions you make will be affected by size and scale. What is the size and scale of your company when considering who to hire? What is the size and scale of your company compared with the company you are considering partnering with? Sure, it might be great to be in business with a national marketing or sales company, but is it better for you to partner with a local marketing firm or outsource to someone with a reputation as a sales guru?

I have to be honest and say that I have found the most successful partnering with smaller entrepreneur types of companies. Certainly, that depends on where you are on a business scale, but for me the right people are those running their own companies that support other businesses. These owners have a lot of expertise and experience in a particular area because they have worked for other companies. Now they are on their own, making their mark on the business world in the way they want to. More often than not, their rates are lower than bigger companies. But the caveat is, like you, these people are looking to build *relationships* rather than looking at you as just a number. And relationships lead to true partnerships, which is always better for business.

WIN-WIN

Another reason I prefer to partner with smaller businesses as vendors is because doing so creates a win-win.

First of all, from a fee perspective, what they charge fits your business and is warranted. Small businesses can also be more flexible in what they charge because they don't have a ton of overhead. Both businesses will have skin in the game, which means a win-win.

Another win-win happens when both businesses are promoting each other (which small businesses are known to do) and trying to find customers for each other. Personal introductions to other businesses and potential clients mean that both sides are growing because both businesses are championing each other.

Here is yet another win-win. The larger a business is, the more self-focused it is on what the business is offering and how it can grow. However, smaller entrepreneur companies are always looking to network because networking is one of the quickest paths to business growth. If you contact a small company regarding supplying a particular product, but they cannot help you, chances are they know a business that can. In my world I tend to remember companies who make connections for my business but don't directly benefit from doing so. When the time comes, I'll go back to that original company to see if we can do business together.

Here are a couple of great reasons for partnering with a smaller entrepreneurial company that creates a win-win:

- Smaller companies tend to be community focused. From a business point of view, if there is a "positive" to take from the COVID-19 pandemic, it is that communities realized just how vital small business are to their neighborhoods and cities. A November 2020 LegalZoom article noted, "About 67 cents of every dollar spent at a small business stays and circulates in the local community."[23]

- Business partnerships are free. And the benefit of "free" is word-of-mouth advertising of one company on behalf of another. The biggest benefit is the word of mouth from the owner

---

23   Anne Brennan, "Small Business Saturday: How Business Owners Can Make the Most of It," LegalZoom, updated May 11, 2023, https://www.legalzoom.com/articles/why-small-business-saturday-is-more-important-than-ever-during-the-pandemic.

to their customers. This also benefits the local community because partnerships between businesses can quickly solve a need for customers.

STRATEGIES

As you think about companies you can partner with, before you reach out to any of them, it is important to have some strategies in place. Here are a few to consider:

RESEARCH

Think about the products and services your business offers. Then ask yourself, What do you offer, and what is missing that you can't afford to do? (Hint: Remember to ask yourself this question in terms of your niche-specific business.) What companies can you partner with that offer what you can't? Who do you need to contact to start the partnership conversation? Note: When you find out who this person is, be prepared with your "business pitch" and how a partnership can create a win-win.

INCENTIVIZE

You can offer discounts on your products and services or some type of reward to other businesses for customers who come your way via a recommendation. You can also offer free samples, consultations, or small gifts and thank-you cards to show your appreciation. With a business partnership, one partner has a solution that a customer needs, which creates a win-win-win!

LOCAL CHARITIES

Partnerships are not limited to businesses; they can include nonprofits as well. There's an old saying that heartstrings are connected to purse strings. Donating to a local charity, sports league, or other nonprofit gives you a tax write-off and free advertisement (your win) while the charity gains monetarily (their win).

EMPLOYEES

Here is a novel idea.

Most often, companies view employees as order-taker people; the boss says this, and the employee does that. The problem is that the employees' contributions to the business can fall into the expected-and-routine trap. But what if you, the business owner, were to see your employees as business partners? You will then see these people as "contributors" rather than someone who is a "taker" (i.e., they are given a paycheck, which means they are taking money out of the company).

There is a huge beneficial reason for seeing employees as business partners. Doing so leads to an understanding that everyone has a shared purpose and a common goal—everyone has skin in the game—to work toward. And when the goal is reached, everyone should benefit. Having an employees-as-business-partners mindset will help you to realize the important insights that are beneficial to your company's overall success. Seeing employees as partners will also help you take a more serious look at what they are saying that you can implement as opposed to you being the know-it-all owner. Recognizing an employee's input and contribution will create a sense of personal ownership and responsibility toward their individual jobs and the company as a whole.

On a more personal note, I've found that having this mindset toward my employees has created friendships and relationships that foster loyalty to me and my company. My employees understand what I have gone through and what I am doing to grow the business, and they willingly join me.

As a business owner, I encourage you to think about everyone you hire—via outsourcing or in person—as a business partner who is an extension of yourself and your business. Whomever you hire is there to save you time and money, which will lead to you having more time and money. As the old saying goes, *time is money*, and the right hiring decision will save you time that can be spent on growing your business, which will equate to more money.

There is a familiar saying that oftentimes applies to business: it's not what you know; it's who you know. That's the topic for the next chapter.

PAT'S POINTS TO PONDER

- Depending on what stage you are in the business, a business partner, such as the marketing firm I hired, can be a real asset. However, you don't want to bring in any partner—you want to bring in the *right* one.

- Before making a decision, ask yourself, "If I outsource an area of my business, will doing so save me time and money?"

- Just like you, people who are running their own small businesses are looking to build *relationships* rather than looking at you as just a number. And relationships lead to true partnerships, which is always better for business.

- Seeing employees as business partners means that everyone has a shared purpose and a common goal—everyone has skin in the game—to work toward.

CHAPTER 11

The Kevin Bacon Game Also Works in Business

Six degrees of separation ... means that a very small number of people are linked to everyone else in a few steps, and the rest of us are linked to the world through those special few.

—MALCOLM GLADWELL

H ave you ever run into a friend somewhere you didn't expect to? Or met someone new and found out you had friends or family in common? No doubt this has happened to you, and you might have said, "What a small world!"

There's an expression that describes the small world in which we live. It's called "six degrees of separation." You've probably heard of this popular terminology that was first explored by psychologist Stanley Milgram in the 1950s. The idea is that all people throughout the world are just six or fewer social connections away from one another.

If you've watched movies over the years, then the name Kevin Bacon is a familiar one. Kevin Norwood Bacon is an American actor and one of Hollywood's most endearing people. His films include the musical drama film *Footloose* (1984), the controversial historical conspiracy legal thriller *JFK* (1991), the legal drama *A Few Good Men* (1992), the historical docudrama *Apollo 13* (1995), and the mystery drama *Mystic River* (2003).[24]

Because Kevin is so popular in Hollywood, a game has been invented with his name, "Six Degrees of Kevin Bacon." Because of his prolific career and diverse ranges of characters, anyone in Hollywood can be linked to another in a handful of steps based on their association with Bacon. The name of the game derives from the idea of six degrees of separation. Although he was initially dismayed by the game, the meme stuck, and Bacon eventually embraced it, forming the charitable initiative SixDegrees.org, a social networking service intended to link people and charities to each other.[25]

While I don't have the popularity that Kevin Bacon does, I can tell you that in my business—and in most businesses—almost all of my current relationships, clients, and business development have happened because of the "six degrees of separation" idea. I would meet someone who could then put me in touch with someone else, which would lead to a meeting with another person, who could then set up a meeting with someone else. And if I hadn't made a connection with one individual that led to another, etc., my business wouldn't be where it is today.

---

24   Kevin Bacon, Wikipedia, accessed November 9, 2022, https://en.wikipedia.org/wiki/Kevin_Bacon.

25   Kevin Bacon, Wikipedia.

SALES 101

Making connections is considered Sales 101 in the business world. I'm constantly reminding my team, and myself, that we never turn down a meeting, no matter how insignificant it might seem.

In the early days of growing my company, I would meet people, and it was pretty obvious they were trying to sell me something. But I would always meet the person with the idea of trying to understand their business and who their clients were. Even if this person had a product or service I wasn't interested in, I would listen to learn, and I cannot tell you the number of times these meetings led to connecting with other people who eventually became my clients. As well, many of these meetings became a win-win; the person I met with would get my business, and he would connect me to someone with whom I could do business.

Always keep in mind that you may not have a direct connection that directly supports your business or presents a sales opportunity, but most business development happens because you continue to listen for when "opportunity knocks," and you stay open-minded. A meeting or a connection may take you down a path that you didn't realize you could go down as a business owner. But because that meeting spurred an opportunity, that is how introductions are made. I know that in my business, opportunities happen because of two, three, four, or maybe six degrees of separation from a meeting that happened a couple of years ago.

SIX DEGREES AND NETWORKING

If you think about it, six degrees of separation happens because of networking. Networking is all about making connections. When two people meet, most often in informal settings, they exchange information and ideas, looking to see if there are commonalities or special interests. In business circles, professionals use networking to expand their circles of acquaintances and potential customers, to find job opportunities, or simply to exchange business cards and information.

The problem I see with most networking is that people focus on themselves and how they can benefit—what can I get out of this connection? In reality, networking should be about finding ways to help others. And that tends to come back to you in a positive way.

When preparing for a network event—or even finding yourself in an impromptu meeting—it's imperative to learn about others. Yes, you want to develop a relationship, but it's best to do so with a "How can I help you?" mentality. If your sole focus is on introducing a product or service, or on making a sale, others will instinctively know this, and you will turn them off. Think about it: Have you ever gone to a showroom and you want to browse around, only to have a salesperson follow you around like a puppy dog? I'm sure you were turned off and maybe even left the store earlier than planned.

Here's a better mindset to have when attending a networking event. If Jim Smith was in a meeting that you attended, and you felt you could do business with him down the road, you could introduce him to Sally Jones, who had something Jim would be interested in. You have just made two successful connections that could pay dividends down the road.

The reason you can make this connection is because you've learned to listen—listen to what other business owners need or have to offer. Always be willing to make business connections when appropriate. That's what networking is all about, and people in networks are only separated by six degrees. So always be polite and respectful. Don't try to sell yourself or oversell what you or your company can do. Don't be afraid to ask for an introduction or for help, and always remember to do the same for someone else. You never know when "business karma" will come into play. Over the course of my business career, I have found these five points to keep in mind for networking and business development:

Be who you are.

I've noticed that, at times, people try to be like chameleons; they try to blend in to find connections, and in doing so they are being someone they are not. "Fake it till you make it" is no way to act in business. It might seem like a good way to make initial inroads; however, I've always found that authenticity is the key to viable and long-lasting connections and relationships. Being yourself means you are accessible and relatable to others. I have also found that it's good to have a story or two ready to share about myself or a business transaction. I've learned that personal stories connect emotionally, and emotional connections are the best way to keep me in the mind of someone else, long after we have parted company. And I never forget to smile. Not a cheesy type of smile but one that makes me and the other person relax and approachable.

Connect, connect, connect.

Networking is about making connections, not about making a sale. Sales come when there is a need that must be met. When networking, I focus on building relationships, not sales. I've found that one of the keys to connecting is my ability to listen, not my ability to talk. There's a life coaching term called "active listening" in which you are hearing the person's words—you hear what they are saying—but you're listening for what they really need. For instance, every business owner will say, "I need more business." However, what a particular business owner might really need is to manage their finances better, which will increase their profit margin.

Think about this: experts say that up to 93 percent of communication is nonverbal. That's why active listening is so important. Active listening includes listening to the other person's tone of voice, watching for their energy and passion or lack thereof, and being in tune with their body language.

I've learned to talk about half as much as the other person. When I do talk, I ask engaging, open-ended questions because I want to know more about that person and their business. Certainly, I talk about myself and my business, but I'm looking for shared interests, common goals, and other connections. I'm looking to build a rapport that can be continued down the road.

Make personal connections.

While technology gives us lots of tools to connect remotely, I tell my team that is nothing like having a face-to-face meeting. Deeper and more lasting connections that are made in person are far more noteworthy. It is also easier to be funny, when appropriate, which is great for building relationships.

Make it memorable.

I know that the final moments I, or a team member, spend with a new or long-term client are crucial. I remind my team to make eye contact, express their gratitude for the meeting, and exchange business cards, phone numbers, etc. I also remind them that the key is to write something down that will jog their memory about the who, what, and where of this meeting.

Follow up/reconnect.

In my team meetings, we ask each other, "Who do you need to follow up or reconnect with?" This might be via an email, phone call, text message, or social media. But I caution you: don't overdo it. If you're like me, there are individuals or companies that I've connected with, and all of a sudden, I am getting daily text messages or emails. Don't be the person who overdoes connecting and drives the other person crazy! It's the quickest way to get deleted or blocked.

TRANSACTIONAL VERSUS RELATIONAL

In my team meetings, we've talked a lot about the difference between being "transactional" versus "relational."

Transactional people are focused on the sale or what they can get out of the meeting. In essence they are saying, "Hey, I've got a widget to sell, and here's our selling price. Do you need it? If not, can you introduce me to someone who does?" There is no personal connection, no relationship established.

Relational people are looking to build a relationship first before business is conducted. "Hi, I'm Pat, and it's great to get to know you. I'm the owner of the Leap Companies, and I'm in the restaurant furniture and recruiting businesses. I really like your business and business model, and I was wondering if there is anything I can do to help you increase your business." After your initial introduction, it's important to listen. Listen to their reply, certainly, but listen for their energy level, their tone of voice, and their body language. With 93 percent of communication being nonverbal, you'll be able to gauge someone's interest by listening to their entire being. And when you find someone who is interested in a deeper conversation, be sure to let them know what you can do for them and how you can help. Whether initially or in the near future, the person will certainly come back to you to find out more about what you do and how they can do business with your company.

In my company, we try to build a foundation first—how we can best serve the other person or company—then build a relationship. This allows any transaction to naturally occur over time. I've never been a hard-core buy-today-or-you'll-lose-out salesperson, and I've told my team never to be this way. There has to be commonality, synergy, and a good fit—a win-win.

Relationship building takes time, and it is always best to have long-term business relationships. Relationships also hinge on a foundation of trust. So always be a person of your word; say what you mean and mean what you say. If for some reason you cannot fulfill your word, be sure to let the other person know what has happened and how you can make amends in the near future.

For example, as you know, a big piece of our company is selling furnishings to the restaurant industry. However, we discovered this was a viable business model because of a couple of meetings I had with a client, but I had no idea what they needed. This person was a great connection, so I wanted to see if there was a mutual business opportunity. But it was this meeting and this client that led me to create our restaurant furnishings division and develop a supply chain. What started out as an I-don't-know-why-I'm-here meeting ended with a new path for business.

When you're growing your business, chances are that family members will come to you looking for a job. But are family members the right people to hire? We'll look at that next.

LEAPING FORWARD ⊕

PAT'S POINTS TO PONDER

- You're only six degrees of separation from your first, or next, business deal.

- Don't turn down a meeting; you never know where it will lead.

- Being yourself leads to trust, and trust is what business deals are founded on.

- Don't be the person who overdoes connecting and drives the other person crazy!

- Meet in person whenever possible and be relationship driven; don't focus on the transaction.

CHAPTER 12

The Pros and Cons of Hiring Family

> If you hire relatives, you'll have a payroll that won't quit.
>
> *—MILTON BERLE*

Before I started Leap Hospitality, I received good insights into what a successful family-run business looks like. Mitzi's family started their music business, Meyer Music, over fifty-five years ago, and it's still going strong, and they've done so through hiring family members for the most part. I studied their business with a lot of admiration, knowing that all of the kids *wanted* to work with their mom and dad and with each other.

The biggest lesson I learned from her family was to separate emotion from business. They were all professional at leaving their "family hat" at the door of the business and conducting business as professionals and employees by working well together. I rarely saw or heard any of the family bring the business into their personal relationships. In my years in business, I can count on three fingers the number of businesses I've known of that have had this type of cohesiveness.

In the early years of my business, I hired my brother to run the sales department. But it didn't work out. The issues weren't personal, nor was there a personality clash. At that time we were focused on driving sales while controlling expenses. My brother was very organized and detail oriented, but as a start-up company, we weren't generating much profit, and we were struggling to manage payroll and other expenses. I also had my own family to take care of.

Letting my brother go was one of the hardest decisions I've ever made. But I gave him a "soft landing" by keeping him on until he found another job that was better suited for him. That's just what he did, and he has flourished! It was rough for both of us, but we are now in a much better place. This decision took a lot of pressure off me, and I've got to give my brother kudos for accepting that difficult situation and for taking the high road.

Have the hard conversation of setting boundaries beforehand.

Chris, who leads our recruiting department, had a similar problem. He brought his brother in to be part of his team; however, a few months later, Chris came to me and said, "It's not working out with my brother. What should I do?" We talked about the good relationship the two of them had, then talked at length about the stress Chris was under, trying to grow profits while controlling expenses. While I could empathize with Chris, I wasn't going to let his brother go; Chris needed to do this himself. Making tough decisions is part of management and part of life.

Here's my advice: if you're going to hire a family member, have the hard conversation of setting boundaries between work and personal relationships *before* bringing in that individual. Whether it's your spouse, brother, sister, son, or daughter, everyone needs to understand that there is a line drawn between being family and being an employee when they walk through the door of your company in the morning. As the owner you need to have thick skin and force yourself to make the distinction between family member and employee at the appropriate times. As well, everyone needs to understand that there's a possibility that things may not work out, whether it's the wrong timing or even the wrong person.

EXTENSION OF FAMILY

When you first start working with your vendors, you'll see them as strictly business partners. But as the relationship develops, you will begin to see them as an extension of your family. You'll get to know these people on a personal level, and you will care about them on this level. Many of our vendors are small businesses that have become integrated with my company, and because of the relationship we have, we can count on each other to be flexible and accommodating and to go out of our way to help if a need or a crisis arises. I see a huge advantage in working with smaller companies, if for no other reason than the personal attention they offer over larger companies.

THE GOOD AND THE NOT SO GOOD

I've often heard this statement, and it bears repeating: the business of business is business. The bottom line is that a business is in business to make money. That's just reality. Having said that, there are some good business reasons for hiring family members, and there are some drawbacks as well.

PROS

One of the best reasons to hire family members is that, first and foremost, you already know this person on a personal level. You know their personality, their work style and habits, and there is a level of synergy between the two of you. There is also an innate sense of trust. As well, you can feel good about helping out by providing a good job. Maybe your family member is just starting their career, and you are giving them the opportunity to prove themselves. Perhaps it's an older family member who is reentering the workforce. And if your goal is to run a family-owned company, then you are creating a business legacy that can be passed on to your kids when the time is right.

Meyer Music, the business of Mitzi's parents, is a great example of this. As they've grown through the years, they have added family members and given people opportunities. Some have worked out and others have not. But "family" is a big part of their culture and story.

Elite Booth, one of my main vendors, is another example of a successful family-run business. The company started around the same time as the Leap Companies, and we have grown together. Over the years I have watched them add family members, and as Matt Reeder, the owner, has told me, "We all know each other, and we know what we are getting."

CONS

As your business grows and evolves, not everyone is going to be flexible. Maybe the business evolves faster than your father's skills, perhaps your nephew isn't adapting to their role, maybe your brother isn't fulfilling his managerial responsibilities. Unless there is a clear understanding that "the business of business is business," I'll guarantee you that emotions will cause problems when difficulties arise. So you have to ask yourself a couple of tough questions: "How will I handle difficulties? How will I handle the situation if I have to fire a family member?"

Keep in mind that it takes maturity and understanding among all the family members, and no one can have the mentality that "I'm family, so I can 'coast' when I want to." If the business is going to thrive, there are times when you'll have to have difficult conversations, which can become even more difficult because of your personal relationships. And these types of conversations can easily spill over outside of business hours. I'm sure you have heard the saying, "Buyer beware." In a family-run business, it's "Family, be aware."

YOUR SPOUSE/PARTNER IS YOUR MOST IMPORTANT BUSINESS PARTNER

I'm going to take a short segue to make a very important point. No matter what type of family business you have, or what family members are involved, it is crucial to every aspect of your business that you have the support of your spouse or partner—something I cannot emphasize enough!

Whether you are married or have a partner, you are both "married" to your business. So you have to take into account their thoughts, views, beliefs, even if they have nothing to do with the actual business. The reason is simple: the business directly affects your relationship.

Is your spouse/partner a risk-taker or a conservative thinker? Do you have open and honest communication, or are there trust issues? No matter what decisions you make, your spouse/partner cannot be left in the dark. That's the quickest way to destroy the relationship *and* the business.

Years ago, when I initially told Mitzi that we were taking out a HELOC as a financial backup for the business, I explained that it was like a rainy-day fund, just in case. She asked a few questions—"It's like an emergency line of credit, right? It's just sitting there, and we won't be paying interest until we used it, is that correct?"—then she agreed. The problem? I quickly maxed out the HELOC because of things I didn't know and couldn't plan for regarding the business.

To her credit, Mitzi never paid the HELOC much attention, partly because she was busy with her own business and partly because she trusted me to not put our family at risk. The dichotomy in our situation was that Mitzi is a conservative thinker, yet she never worried about the extra debt, while I am a risk-taker, but I struggled with constant anxiety over the increased debt load!

What could have been an explosive situation was negated because of Mitzi's trust in me. But I caution you: don't take trust for granted. Don't assume that just because you feel something is worth doing or a risk is worth taking, your spouse/partner is in agreement. Don't assume … communicate. Also, even if your spouse/partner is not involved in the business, if you are questioning something, then run it by your loved one. There are times when they will have a "sixth sense"—an uneasy or a positive feeling—about what you are going to do. When that happens, take their intuition under advisement.

If you're in the planning stages, whether you're purchasing a business or starting one, having some kind of just-in-case nest egg needs to be part of your foundational planning. It is also paramount that you are transparent about the business and the decisions being made and to make the other person's thoughts, views, and opinions part of the process. Sure, we think everything is going to go fine; there is nothing to worry about. But business reality says that we're going to face some curveballs, and we're going to get blindsided at some point.

Having a rainy-day fund will take the pressure off everyone, but the fund needs to have your significant other's or business partner's buy-in. Don't hide what you want to do or are doing. Don't be the person who says I'll do this now and ask for forgiveness later. I can tell you from experience that things will go south pretty quickly. In the past I've started a few business ventures that I didn't involve Mitzi in simply because I didn't want to hear a different viewpoint or opinion. But if I had been smart enough to talk to her, I would have saved myself many heartaches and headaches simply because her opposite nature to mine and her different mindset would have pointed out things I never thought about.

For example, while building the Leap Companies, there were times when Mitzi would tell me something, and I would say, "You're just plain wrong." But after reflecting on what she said, I could see things in a different perspective. Being bullheaded never gets anyone anywhere, and being bullheaded in a marriage is never good.

Over the years I've realized that "opposites *do* attract." In many instances Mitzi has saved me a lot of time, effort, and in some cases money. I've learned that I sometimes need her perspective; otherwise, I would get myself into trouble. Sure, there are times I don't like her answers—and you won't like answers from your significant other or business partner. But if you don't have this person involved on a day-to-day basis, when the unexpected happens, the back-end conversation is not fun! Transparency and honesty will bring about some interesting conversations, and if the business doesn't grow—or even collapses—at least there would have been joint decision-making, so there won't be any finger-pointing.

When I invested in the restaurants in years past, I had to sign a lease that I personally guaranteed. However, I never told Mitzi because I didn't want her to slow down the process. But with the lack of concept for the restaurants to follow and profits never materializing, I was on the financial hook in ways I never dreamed of. Fortunately, I maneuvered through this dicey time in my life, but I was sick to my stomach most days. When I reflect back on that situation, I realize that had I involved Mitzi from the beginning, I never would have invested in the restaurants, and I would have saved a whole lot of time, energy, and money—not to mention the sleepless nights I would not have suffered through.

In business no one can be an island unto themselves. All business owners need the support, insight, and encouragement of like-minded people. Business support groups are a great place to find these people, and we'll discuss that next.

LEAPING FORWARD ⊕↑

PAT'S POINTS
TO PONDER

- When working with family, always separate emotion from business.

- If you're going to hire a family member, have the hard conversation of setting boundaries between work and personal relationships *before* bringing in that individual. Being yourself leads to trust, and trust is what business deals are founded on.

- If the business is going to thrive, there are times when you'll have to have difficult conversations, which can become even more difficult because of your personal relationships.

- Whether you are married or have a partner, you are both "married" to your business. So you have to take into account their thoughts, views, beliefs, even if they have nothing to do with the actual business.

CHAPTER 13

AA for Entrepreneurs: Business Support Groups

Find a group of people who challenge and inspire you, spend a lot of time with them, and it will change your life forever.

—AMY POEHLER

have no doubt that you've heard the phrase "No man is an island" at some point in your life. It grew out of sermon given by seventeenth-century English author John Donne. His original quote was, "No one is self-sufficient; everyone relies on others."[26]

In the business world, both versions are applicable.

When you are first starting to build your business, in some ways you are an island. You're the head of sales, head of product and development, head of marketing and branding, etc. However, when you begin to hire people to fill critical roles, it is easy to maintain an

---

26   Dicitionary.com, "No man is an island," https://www.dictionary.com/browse/no-man-is-an-island.

"island" mentality, thinking that you are the only one who can grow your company. The problem with that mentality is you will remain on your "island" until you realize you must reach out to other business owners and professionals if you want to grow your business beyond your own mindset.

If you are going to grow your company beyond what you know and envision, you have to reach out to like-minded people, and that is when business support groups are invaluable.

Business support groups are not networking groups. They are gatherings of business owners, who may or may not be in the same industry. But what they have in common is the need to "think outside the box" of their own mindset. A common need to talk about struggles, goals, dreams, and plans for the future. The need to develop personally and professionally.

In the early days of growing my business, I didn't see the need for a business support group until I received a chance call from a man who represented an organization called "The Alternative Board." He explained that the mission of the fee-based organization is to gather like-minded businesspeople together in a once-a-month group to talk collectively about our businesses, get recommendations and advice, brainstorm ideas and potential solutions, vent our frustrations and celebrate our successes, and support each other in making decisions. It was always an open forum. After attending a couple of meetings, I realized these groups were akin to having my own board of directors! As a bonus, the individual who spearheaded the organization was a consultant who worked with us one-on-one, whether it be to align personal goals or business goals. This gave all of us a lot of confidence to make decisions that we needed to make.

GETTING UNSTUCK

Oftentimes in business you have hard decisions to make. Do I hire a particular person? Is this contract a good deal for my company? Do I maintain the status quo or try to grow? If you're like me, you feel like you're stuck in the mud, spinning your wheels. However, a business group will help you get unstuck.

A couple of months after joining The Alternative Board organization, the facilitator and participants in the group really pushed me. They challenged me to take action on a particular path I thought was the right one. They instilled confidence in me to make decisions and to move in my chosen direction. I think I already knew I needed to go, but they gave me the confidence to make that move. The time I spent with these people was more than just great for business; it was therapeutic. I was going through probably the hardest time as a business owner, and these people allowed me to talk through whatever I was going through instead of keeping everything bottled up inside of me. Unfortunately, the individual who started that group passed away, and the group soon disbanded.

I was on my own again for about four years, then someone reached out to me with an opportunity to join a different type of group.

The group is made up of specific entrepreneurs called Entrepreneurs' Organization (EO). This is an international entity through which I meet with other business owners once a month. We talk about the big issues we face in business. But we also talk about the small stuff we face individually; the 5 percent of most conversation we wish we could have but have never been able to. We get into deep dives at this level. I've joined this organization twice over the years, and the rewards have been golden.

Over the last three to four years, Leap has matured as a company, with better direction and a clear understanding of what we are doing. And I can definitely say that EO has been integral to our success. Being surrounded by like-minded businesspeople has given me the confidence to make some bold moves and decisions. I've gained insights from these businessmen and have been on the inside to their decision-making process and how they have implemented those decisions. For instance, if I have struggled in making a particular decision, someone will ask, "Well, why is that?" Then we would dig into this together

Being surrounded by like-minded businesspeople has given me the confidence to make some bold moves and decisions.

so that I could determine what was holding me back and what I wanted to do about it. The group is not one for giving advice; they are very gestalt. However, they share their insights, examples, and perspectives, all of which have helped guide me to another level.

The group has also helped me grow as a person versus flying solo in a plane and trying to figure out where I'm going. It is comforting to have a stable group of "copilots" with me that really doesn't cost anything other than the monthly price of the organization.

Another great benefit is having access to business partners that I would not have known otherwise. Someone always knows somebody who knows someone else—just like the "six degrees of separation" I talked about in the last chapter.

PERSONAL FULFILLMENT

One of the great things about joining a business group is the personal growth I have gained, which leads to personal fulfillment. Instead of just doing business for the sake of business, there has to be meaning—personal meaning—to what you are doing. For me, this means I have grown and matured as a person. I have grown and matured as a businessman. My life has purpose, and I'm helping those on my team to have purpose for themselves instead of simply working to earn a living. I have also built a solid reputation in the business world, and am building a legacy business that my kids can take over, if they decide to.

I have always liked the idea of "create, create, create" and then seeing the results of that labor. So having my own business has fulfilled me, whereas if I had worked for somebody else, I probably wouldn't have had that same sense of gratification.

As an entrepreneur you should be able to relate to what I am saying. You are an independent person, someone who wants to make their own path in life. And joining a business group can reaffirm your way of thinking and the way you are made. This can give you an entirely new perspective on everything you do.

SETTING GOALS AND ACCOUNTABILITY

Every personal development coach will tell you the benefit of writing out your personal goals. Every business coach or consultant will also tell you the benefit of writing out your business goals. Although I follow this sage advice all the time, it is not always easy to do, and it can be hard to do so on your own. If you are like me, you feel like you need a coach or a group of friends, or peers to hold you accountable. I am always holding my team accountable, but in many ways, personal and professional, there isn't anyone holding me accountable. So accountability is another benefit of being part of a business group. I have to report back to them on my goals and progress without giving lame excuses. I wake up every day knowing I have to do this. Because I don't like letting others down, I make sure that I'm ready to report back to my business group, knowing they are going to ask me "Did you achieve your action items or not? You said you were going to do x, y, and z by the time we met again. Did you do it? And if you didn't do it, why didn't you do it? But if you did do it, we are here to congratulate you." There are a lot good things to be said about being held accountable.

Speaking of accountability, here are some shocking statistics:[27]

- New research reveals that fewer than one in five people are able to successfully hold others accountable for delivering on expectations in the workplace.

- Partners In Leadership, an accountability training and culture change company, conducted the research, called the Workplace Accountability Study.

- 82% of respondents admitted that they have "limited to no" ability to hold others accountable successfully. On the other hand 91% of respondents said they would rank "improving the ability to hold others accountable in an effective way" as one of the top leadership development needs of their organization.

---

27   Tom Starner, "Study: Workplace Accountability Requires a Specific Strategy," HR Dive, June 2, 2015, https://www.hrdive.com/news/study-workplace-accountability-requires-a-specific-strategy/400130/.

However, there are almost unlimited benefits to having someone or a group of individuals hold you accountable for your actions. Consider the following:

- First and foremost, accountability makes you responsible for your attitudes and actions and keeping your word.

- Being accountable causes you to be a person of integrity.

- Accountability promotes ownership versus playing the "blame game."

- It reduces and can eliminate conflicts.

- Accountability highlights time and effort spent on frivolous activities and unproductive behavior.

- It is a great way to track your progress and gain the confidence of others.

- Accountability inspires self-confidence by noting positive changes and accomplishments.

- It builds self-trust and draws trust from others.

- Accountability supports you in taking new actions while challenging or eliminating what holds you back.

In my life I have found that when I write down my goals and objectives, and I have to show them to someone, I'm going to follow through. For instance, it's easy for me to tell everyone, "I'm going to lose ten pounds." That is a generic statement. But if I say, "I'm going to lose ten pounds in two months, and here's how I'm going to do it," it forces me to a different level of accountability. Like most people, and especially entrepreneurs, this type of challenge brings out the competitive nature in me; if I say I'm going to do something, then I'm going to do it!

THERAPEUTIC AND SELF-FOCUSED

While business groups aren't therapy groups, I can tell you from personal experience there is a therapeutic side to getting something off your chest. This includes frustrations, challenges, problems, and a host of other things. A foundational principle of business groups is being nonjudgmental. Personal and professional issues can easily become intertwined, and those in a business group do their best to maintain objectivity.

Focusing on yourself is another benefit to being part of a business group. Whether in your business or at home, you are constantly serving others. You wear all types of hats—the father hat, the husband hat, the businessman's hat, the leader's hat … you get the picture. As well, most entrepreneurs are type A personalities; as the boss, you are always in the driver's seat. In all the roles you play, it isn't very often that someone asks about you and how you are doing. In a business group, that's exactly what happens: someone asks about *you*. So you can be a little selfish. You can talk about yourself. You can take some time for some self-care.

In my business group, we meet once a month for four hours. No phones to distract us. No computers to monitor. I tell my team that unless the world is burning down, I'm unreachable. Initially, blocking this time was hard, and I felt a little panicked. But I have learned that my business can live without me for four hours, and I always leave these meetings having had time to think, to process, and to become more clearheaded.

I trust you can see the many benefits of being a member of a business support group. If you've already made this commitment, that's great! If you haven't, I challenge you to find a group that will push you to change and grow, personally and professionally. You will be amazed at the success that will come your way!

Just like people, a business needs an identification, something that sets it apart from other companies in the same industry. Your company's culture will do just that, which is the subject of the next chapter.

PAT'S POINTS TO PONDER

- If you are going to grow your company beyond what you know and envision, you have to reach out to like-minded people, and that is when business support groups are invaluable.

- A business support network will push you, instill confidence, and be therapeutic.

- A business group is like having a stable group of "copilots" that doesn't cost anything other than the monthly price of the organization.

- You may be holding your team or suppliers accountable, but who is holding you accountable, personally and professionally, for your attitudes and actions and keeping your word?

CHAPTER 14

Creating a Company Culture

A company's culture is the foundation for future innovation.
An entrepreneur's job is to build the foundation.

—BRIAN CHESKY

A s we move into this chapter, I'd like you to keep the following in mind: You are your company, and your company is you. You reflect your company, and your company reflects you. Here's what I mean. Are you laid-back and adaptable? Are you focused and hard driving? Are you fun loving? Serious? A black-and-white thinker, or do you allow for gray areas? It is your temperament, **The tone you set will create a company culture that your business operates by.** your personality, and your character that will set the tone for your company. And the tone you set will create a company culture that your business operates by.

Depending on what stage your business is in will determine how your company culture will manifest itself. For example, if yours is a start-up company, then you are your company's culture. But as you add personnel and team members, it becomes more important to "memorialize" what that culture needs to be. By "memorialize" I mean *documented*.

In the start-up phase, you are focused on growing your business. You are working to reach customers, to meet their needs, to establish finances, along with a whole host of other issues that need your attention. But as you add personnel, they will challenge you, directly or indirectly. At this point, it's important that you establish your company's culture so that everyone knows how business is conducted. Trust me, this takes time and effort.

In my case it wasn't until year sixteen of my business that I decided to step back and take an in-depth look at my company's culture, even though I had been contemplating doing so for the past three or four years. I would do a little bit here and there, with limited attention. Then I realized my company had needed a defined identity, and identity comes with establishing a company culture.

One of the key criteria in determining your company culture is deciding to "take your hands off the wheel," which I will talk about in the next chapter. Once you make that decision, you need to work on this culture process and core values and document them because as your company moves forward and grows, these are much hard to define and control.

WHAT IS COMPANY CULTURE?

You might be wondering if there is a definition for "company culture." It can be described as a company's shared goals and values. Company culture can also be called *workplace culture*. It details how employees work together, the company's policies and procedures, and how decisions are made.

Some companies have a traditional and conservative culture, such as banks and law firms. These industries are governed by regulations that must be followed precisely. These companies often have a top-down management style, with decisions made by upper management. Other companies, such as advertising and design, focus on creative interests and are more likely to have a relaxed culture, where many people have input into how the company operates.

No matter how you define and describe and what you include in your company's culture, what will make it successful is the fact that it truly represents the way you do business day in and day out.

For my business, I decided to hire a third-party individual who met with me, then my team and me, to create our company culture. It is truly a collaborative effort to determine who we were and what makes our company special and what we wanted to be. We started with defining our core values as a company. That is something that becomes very important as your business grows. The beauty of defining our core values is that it made each of us duplicable and accountable because company culture is driven by core values. This is important because, whether an employee is new or has been with the company for a number of years and whether a client is new or has been doing business with us for a while, everyone knows what we stand for and how we do business. And one of the great benefits of creating company culture is having a living document both employees and customers could read and easily understand.

I would suggest not waiting as long as I did to create your company culture, even if you are a solopreneur. However, when you actually sit down to create your company culture will partly depend on the number of staff and employees you have. When you start your company, you are more focused on creating a strategy that works for gaining clients. But once your business starts to grow, you want to establish your company's core values and culture so that you're not getting sidetracked trying to be "all things to all people." Instead, defining your company's core values and culture are key to helping both you and staff and employees determine if you are the right fit for each other and for clients and customers to determine if they want to do business with your company.

WHAT TO INCLUDE

As I've noted, company culture is unique to each business. However, there are some commonalities that can be used as a starting point. I think these ten points that are defined by LumApps are an excellent place to start:[28]

1. Decide What Your Ideal Company Culture Looks Like

2. Compare Ideal Company Culture to the Existing One

3. Ask Employees for Input

4. Encourage Work-Life Balance to Reduce Stress

5. Make Sure Employees Know Your Expectations

6. Hire Candidates for Culture First

7. Use Digital Tools and Digital Workplace

8. Recognize Employee Achievements

9. Remind Employees That Their Work Matters

10. Create Opportunities for Employees to Build Relationships

---

28 Antoine Pourron "10 Steps to Build a Successful Company Culture," LumApps, accessed November 12, 2022, https://www.lumapps.com/employee-experience/how-to-build-company-culture/.

CULTURE AND ACCOUNTABILITY

While every company will have its own culture, all company cultures should point to one thing: accountability. In my view, accountability is key to business success.

To state the obvious, COVID-19 has upended the way businesses are run permanently. According to an article from the Wharton School of Business, "Office vacancy rates increased significantly during the COVID-19 pandemic, reaching a high of 17.2 percent in the third quarter of 2021. While many companies are calling workers back into the office this year, full occupancy is unlikely. Workers have proven they can function remotely, and they are demanding their employers keep the option of remote or hybrid work."[29]

In another article from the research firm McKinsey, "80 percent of people questioned report that they enjoy working from home. Forty-one percent say that they are more productive than they had been before and 28 percent that they are as productive."[30]

While these statistics are great to know, as the business owner, how do you hold your employees and team members accountable to complete their work? How do you know that someone is showing up in a virtual meeting or coming into the office part time, ready to go? But as soon as they leave a virtual meeting or at home during normal business hours, how do you know they don't have an "out of sight, out of mind" mentality? Certainly, you can accept that the virtual world is the new norm. However, at the end of the day, the company

---

29   Angie Basiouny, "What's Going to Happen to All Those Empty Office Buildings?" Knowledge at Wharton, February 28, 2022, https://knowledge.wharton.upenn.edu/article/whats-going-to-happen-to-all-those-empty-office-buildings/.

30   Brodie Boland et al., "Reimagining the Office and Work Life after COVID-19," McKinsey & Company, June 8, 2020, https://www.mckinsey.com/capabilities/people-and-organizational-performance/our-insights/reimagining-the-office-and-work-life-after-covid-19.

has to make payroll, and as the owner you feel the full weight of that responsibility.

The last thing you want to suspect your employees of is being lazy. This is exactly why there is a need to emphasize the importance of accountability. When you create this type of culture, everyone within the company proactively takes responsibility.

CULTURE AND TRUSTWORTHINESS

I have always felt that accountability and trustworthiness go hand in hand; it's hard to grow as a company if you can't trust each other. Trustworthiness feeds into accountability because everyone knows the other person is going to do their job, eliminating any worries. As well, people can be trusted to make the right decisions and to get help when needed.

If you think about the idea trustworthiness being part of your company culture, you need to know there is an irony involved. In all likelihood you will have to allow your team members to fail in certain instances and let them learn from their mistakes and come up with their own lessons. As the owner you cannot—and must not—get in the middle of everything. The more you're in the middle, the less you're showing that you trust those who work for you to make the right decision. Certainly, there are times when you will need to correct mistakes that others have made, but do so in a way that doesn't shame or belittle. You don't want to create an atmosphere where people are afraid to make—and admit—mistakes. Instead, help that person realize and understand what went wrong and why, then figure out a solution and a way to prevent the same thing from happening in the future. This is taking a "coach approach" rather than being a feared dictator. Coaching an individual through their mistakes builds trust and accountability and gives the person the confidence to move forward.

Yes, this approach might cost your company some money, so you have to know which mistakes are tolerable and which ones are too big to ignore. You have to "pick your battles" in determining when to get involved and how much of your involvement is needed. And never forget that you, the company owner, have made your share of mistakes. Being humble, forthright, and transparent is key to building trust.

LESSON LEARNED

I've made my own hiring mistakes, which had big impacts on the company.

We looked at expanding our logistics division, and I brought somebody in to help lead the sales effort. Unfortunately, the rails were falling off pretty quickly, and I let it continue and didn't coach this individual the right way.[31] But I also didn't let this person go soon enough. I had to own the mistake and also admit this individual was going to be a culture disruptor, even though they had been with us for a full year. Sadly, everyone on my team already knew this! So I had to own my mistake and apologize to my team, then I reiterated that they had permission to come to me anytime they felt someone or something was wrong. This mistake cost me a pretty penny, but it was important for my team to see me bounce back quickly because my response would determine their response.

---

31 The "right way" to coach is what fits the other person the best and not necessarily the best fit for you.

LACK OF TRUST

It is easy to identify a lack of trust within a company. The atmosphere is one of fear. Water cooler meetings are held to discuss how to acknowledge a mistake without someone being demoted or losing their job. Your staff and employees cannot be afraid of mistakes, and if they are, then you need to find out why and rectify the situation.

Over the years I have seen cover-ups in companies that become culture killers—and even company killers. It is much easier to say, "I made a mistake, but here is a solution" or "I've made a mistake, and I need some help to rectify it." Mistakes that are covered up are bound to rear their ugly heads sooner or later. So it's best to figure out what to do immediately so that the mistake doesn't grow exponentially.

As the owner of my company, I don't like it when someone comes to me and says they made a mistake, then asks, "What should I do?" This shows me that person isn't willing to take ownership or responsibility. Granted, there are extenuating circumstances, but overall when someone asks me that question, they are telling me they don't know how to "think on their feet," that they don't understand their job or what it entails, and they are not thinking two steps ahead. Those who work for you should be critical thinkers, which is another reason why accountability, trust, and understanding a company's culture and core values are so important.

A MIRRORED REFLECTION

Now it's time for you to take a look in the mirror.

The old adage "the buck stops here" applies to you, the owner of your company. Your staff and employees will mirror what you demonstrate. If someone isn't measuring up to your company's culture and core values, it is your job either to coach them to success or to determine if it's time for you to part ways. That is the only way you are going to control your company's culture.

Also, if *you* are not living and breathing your company's culture, then don't expect your staff and employees to do what you won't do. It is up to you to set the expectations every day and every time you interact with staff, employees, clients, and customers.

Here is what the company culture looks like at Leap Companies and what we hold sacred:

Journey: Each team member, vendor, client, or candidate has their own personal journey. It is our mission at Leap to help fulfill and be a part of that journey in the most impactful way, whether it's scaling your concept, promoting your ideas, fulfilling a new career, or building out your company's team. Each individual or company has their own journey they are on, and we aim to be a small part of it in a meaningful, positive way.

Urgent Persistence	We take initiative and push through to the desired result quickly every time.
Genuine Relationships	We humanize work with genuine care and compassion for others over the long term.
Trustworthy	We do what we say and own it with confident transparency.
Forward-Thinking	We don't dwell on the negative and are proactive and solution-oriented.

When working with our third party, we developed these as a team, which I found fascinating because we didn't discuss any of this ahead of time. I wrote out seven or eight core values that I thought were good, and these four were on my list. But my team developed them without much guidance from me. In doing so I realized that we had a culture but had never defined it. I tell you this to say that your company might be in the same position as well. However, in defining your company's culture, you move it from the abstract this-is-what-I-think-it-is to something that is formal that everyone knows to be true.

Urgent Persistence

We are not passive or passive aggressive. We don't take no or failure as an answer, but we keep pushing for the right answer. What I mean is we are always problem-solving and figuring out the next steps. Within our project management, we maintain a sense of urgency on behalf of the client, looking to do what is right and best for them and not having a lackadaisical approach.

Genuine Relationships

In everything we do, whether it be for a team member or a client, when we "humanize" ourselves versus standing behind the image of a company, we show genuine care and compassion for others over the long term, and that always works out. We work hard on getting to know the person or people we are working with on a personal basis so we can understand their desires and goals as opposed to trying to sell a service or product first. Cultivating relationships has been the biggest value to my company. Getting to know a person means we are genuine in our approach. So we empathize "humanizing yourself" in team meetings, which is a big part of who we are as a company.

When I say, "Humanizing," I mean that we are genuine, open, and transparent. For instance, by going to our website and clicking on "About Us," you'll see pictures of my team and me in casual environments. Or descriptions tell who we are, our interests, and something we want to share with the world.

Trustworthy

I've talked a lot about trustworthiness, but being trustworthy is akin to transparency. As a company, "we are who we are."

Forward-Thinking

This is the ability to be innovative. We think two steps ahead, always driving forward versus thinking about the past. The past is what it is, and we can either cower from our mistakes or be "full of ourselves" because of our success.

PLAYING OUT

You might be wondering how these values play out in the real world. Here's an example.

The Cordish Companies have been our longest-standing client. Over time they have really leaned on us to ensure that we met our project budgets and timelines. This has happened because we established three of our company values—genuine relationships, trustworthy, and forward-thinking—from the very start. However, without us being urgent and persistent throughout the time we have done business together for all of their projects, it is doubtful they would still be our clients today.

Over time we have built a transparent relationship together. Doing so meant that when mistakes happened on any level (e.g., missing a deadline or ordering the wrong product), we had built a strong enough relationship that meant we would own our mistakes and come up with an appropriate solution. Both companies know that we have each other's back. When problems arise, one or both companies will resolve them. On my company's end, we make sure their timeline and budget are met. On their end they might be able to extend a deadline or offer to cover a portion of any costs.

Whether it's with the Cordish Companies or another client, when facing a problem, "forward-thinking" is always in play. It is easy to dwell on a mistake or bemoan a mishap. But how does that resolve anything? We can always review what went wrong *after* the problem is fixed to make sure the same thing doesn't happen again. Even when my company is not at fault, there are times when we eat the cost because it's the best way forward. "There is always a way forward" is one of my company's mantras, and it is the reason why we continue to grow and why we have long-standing clients like the Cordish Companies.

MAINTAINING FOCUS

Being in your position as the owner, I fully understand all the responsibilities that you have. The last thing you need to waste time worrying about is what your employees are doing or not doing and taking time to manage policies and procedures. If that is the case, then in my opinion you have the wrong staff and employees working for you. To me, this is pretty cut and dry. That's why having goals and expectations clearly set up front—which is what having a company culture will help you do—is so important, especially in today's society when many people are working remotely.

Here is a stark truth: if you suspect that someone is not doing their job, that they're not adding the value that they are capable of, then you probably don't have the right employee. It's always the *C* that takes up the most time and effort because they need too much hand-holding, while the *A* players are pretty much self-sufficient. So take a good look at who is taking up most of your time, and ask yourself why that is happening. Your answer should then tell you the next steps to take.

QUIET QUITTING

You need to be focused on what ownership is supposed to focus on—things like how to grow the company, working with top-echelon clients, strategic planning, and more. That's why you need staff and employees who take initiative and responsibility. Unfortunately, there is a what I would call a "business disease" infecting all industries. It's called "quiet quitting." I'm sure you've heard this term. Quiet quitting means that someone is not ready to outright quit their job, but they have "quit" the idea of going above and beyond what is expected. The individual still performs their duties, but they are no longer subscribing to the hustle mentality that is necessary to be successful.

While I understand that a job shouldn't be all consuming of one's time and attention, in my view—and I'm sure I'll ruffle some feathers while others will completely agree—quiet quitting is just an excuse *not* to do the extra work needed to move from being a *C* player to an *A* player. This is an unfortunate consequence of remote work or hybrid work—part time at the office and part time working from home. Our current work environment makes it easier for people to do the bare minimum and still survive in a company, especially a larger one. But this is much more difficult to do in a smaller company because each person is critical to making the company run smoothly.

The concept of quiet quitting is foreign to me, and I dare say it should be to you as a business owner. I have always been in either a new position within a company or now owning my own company, in which I have had to create something from nothing to turn a thought or idea into something tangible. When working for someone else, I was most often hired for a brand-new position and had to create my own job description and figure out how I could add value to the company. And there are only two ways to add value: either through sales growth or improving processes and creating efficiencies that lowers expenses. So I'm here to tell you in no uncertain terms, if your staff and employees are not doing one of these two things, then they are probably quiet quitting. Your team's whole function should be in one of those two buckets and to think that way. If not, your company's life might be short-lived. As a hyperbole example, an employee might be a mail clerk whose job is to deliver the mail on time. But once that is determined, the next job is to figure out how to deliver mail to offices in a unique and more timely fashion. The goal for the clerk is to make themselves stand out so that others notice. That's the best way to add value to a company and the surest way to promotion. That's also the difference between being proactive and reactive, something that quiet quitting doesn't acknowledge.

WHEN TO HIRE

A huge part of your ability to maintain focus on your ownership responsibilities is by hiring the right people at the right time. But how do you know the time is right to start hiring? Here are three good indicators:

1. Customer Service Slips

If you're not meeting your customer's needs, then you've got too much on your plate. And the last thing you need is for customers to start complaining. You could tell them, "You'll get right on it," but is that really your job? Besides that, as soon as you hang up, countless other things will demand your attention. To use an analogy, when you have too many plates spinning and you're the only one spinning them, you're putting your business at risk, and it's time to hire someone or outsource some of the work.

If you've heard the term "churn rate," then you know it is the rate of attrition or customer churn, at which customers stop doing business with an entity.[32] In business, churn rate is the opposite of retention and measures the rate at which customers sever their relationships with you. As the owner, if your company's churn rate is too high, then your customer service is too low, and it's time to look at what positions that you need to give up and let someone else fill them.

2. Feeling Overwhelmed

Even if your business is growing, if you're taking too much time off, or spending too much time procrastinating about decisions, then you are overwhelmed. You can identify with the phrase "overworked and underpaid." You may not be ready to hire a full-time employee, but you can consider bringing on a

---

32   Jake Frankenfield, "Churn Rate: What It Means, Examples, and Calculations," Investopedia, updated May 18, 2022, https://www.investopedia.com/terms/c/churnrate.asp.

freelancer or someone from a temp agency. This will allow you to work *on* the business instead of *in* the business.

3. Turning Down Offers

Your business is like having a newborn—both have an insatiable appetite! Your business is "fed" with new customers, clients, or through the products and services you offer. But if keep turning down new business, it might be because you are the "chief cook and bottle washer." It's true that it takes money to hire someone, and you might be reluctant to spend precious finances. But as the old age states, "Sometimes you have to spend money to make money."

Always remember this: if you have been working with a customer and you need to transition that valued business relationship to a new employee, you must stay involved during the transition stage. Be involved on the initial calls so that the customer or client is comfortable working with your new hire. As well, you should always personally introduce the person taking over from you and express your confidence in their business experience and their ability to work well in the business relationship. Both new hire and customer or client need to know that you fully support this new relationship.

MY EXPERIENCE

Over the years it's helped me to realize that when I felt like the day to day was going through me too much, it was time to bring in new people so that the process could work on its own. Bringing new people on board always helps push my company forward. At times I get anxious in knowing I've got to cover their overhead costs. But new hires always help my company respond and execute faster, which is a great way of saving money and increasing profits in the long run.

A word of caution.

I've seen people try to grow their companies too fast and add too much overhead. So there is a fine line to walk, one that only you can define. It has taken me sixteen years to finally have a core team that executes properly. But now I don't have to touch every part of the business. Keep in mind that having the confidence to know when and who to hire comes down to how risk oriented you are and your ability to make decisions without knowing the outcome.

For your business to continually grow, you have to give up some of your control. But how do you do that? We'll look at this in the next chapter.

PAT'S POINTS TO PONDER

- Defining your company's core values and culture is key to helping both you and your staff and employees determine if you are the right fit for each other, for clients, and for customers to determine if they want to do business with your company.

- As you add personnel, they will challenge you, directly or indirectly. At this point it's important that you establish your company's culture so that everyone knows how business is conducted.

- Accountability and trustworthiness go hand in hand; it's hard to grow as a company if you can't trust each other.

- Mistakes that are covered up are bound to rear their ugly heads sooner or later. So it's best to figure out what to do immediately so that the mistake doesn't grow exponentially.

- If *you* are not living and breathing your company's culture, then don't expect your staff and employees to do what you won't do.

- If you suspect that someone is not doing their job, that they're not adding the value that they are capable of, then you probably don't have the right employee.

- If you have been working with a customer and you need to transition that valued business relationship to a new employee, you must stay involved during the transition stage.

CHAPTER 15

When to Take Your Hands off the Wheel

f you want your business to grow past you, you have to decide when and how you can live with management and decisions that take place outside you. In other words you have to let other people take control of aspects of your business if you truly want it to grow. That's just the plain truth.

Now I get it. Your business is your baby. Whether your company is in the start-up stages or your business is on stable financial footing and growing, either way, you are the one who has had extra-long days and sleepless nights. You have given your company its name and branding, and you have done every job associated with your company;

you have had your hands in everything! So who knows your company and what it needs better than you?

Taking your hand off the wheel doesn't mean you are giving up control of your company to someone else; doing that would simply make you an employee. However, in order to begin to scale your business, it has to operate without you being the center of its universe. So repeat after me, "I need to surrender my need to be the center of my business. I'm willing to no longer be the center of my business. I choose to give up being the center of my business." How does that feel? Scary? Freeing? Either way, I understand. As an entrepreneur building your business is both scary and freeing, but if you truly want to grow your business, it requires you to take your hands off the wheel and bring in others to help you. You have to give up control. Your long-term goal is to build a business that runs by itself, with or without you, day in and day out. Why is this so important? Because you cannot grow in your current markets or expand into other market sectors or industries if you solely focus on the day to day of your business.

Taking your hand off the wheel doesn't mean you are giving up control of your company to someone else.

Here's another caveat: your business is much more salable in the future if it runs without you. No matter if you're in the start-up phase or running a mature business, at some point you'll want to sell your company, so you should start with the "end in mind."

Freedom is another huge benefit to giving up some of the control. You might be in the throes of the long-days-and-short-nights phase of growing your business. And if you aren't, you can certainly recall those days than ran into one another for weeks, months, and even years. Having the freedom to step back or a while to enjoy life and to rethink your business plan and prospects is like having a pocket full of good: it's priceless.

WHAT DOES IT LOOK LIKE?

So what does taking your hands off the wheel look like?

First of all, take a detailed inventory of the jobs you currently do in your business. Now ask yourself, What are you passionate about? Do you like doing sales calls? Do you prefer working with established clients? Are you a "numbers" person? When you figure out what you're passionate about, you also know what you *aren't* passionate about. These are the areas in which hiring someone else starts to make sense. For example, I know a guy who runs a business that he simply couldn't grow. He had the education and experience, but no matter what he tried, his business wouldn't grow. So he hired a branding and marketing expert, and a year later his sales tripled. Another businessman had all kinds of sale and profits, but whenever he compiled his monthly statements, the totals didn't reflect what he thought the business should be earning. So he hired an accountant to run the business's finances, and the owner is now more than pleased with the company's bottom line.

Here's a different take. Perhaps you have been working with a particular client who brings you a lot of business, but you really don't get along with that individual. Hiring another account manager to you can introduce your client to makes sense.

Creating new processes and procedures that allow you to take your hands of the wheel will cause you some anxious moments in the beginning. At the outset, you will both have your hands on the wheel—in fact, you will feel like you're doing two jobs for a short time! But as confidence and relationships grow for both of you, you will soon take a hands-off approach. So be aware of how you feel, and be aware of how your new hire feels. You don't want to hover or smother. And your new hire doesn't want to be hovered over or smothered. Keep in mind that the size of the business will determine how short or long the transition period lasts.

When you are ready to hand over some of your responsibility to another person, whether an outside vendor or an employee, you will be adding to your overhead expenses. This means you will need to generate more income, or you may need to find an area in which you can cut back, including your own income. So remind yourself that you are reinvesting in your business for long-term gain. To use a sports analogy, this is "short-term pain for long-term gain."

HOW IT WORKS

As a business owner, it is your job to know when to hire others and for what roles. This is akin to juggling balls in the air; if you have too many balls moving all at once, you are bound to drop one or two. In business, you don't want that to happen.

One of the first things to do is to define "roles and responsibilities." Roles refer to a job position, while responsibilities refer to the tasks and duties that describe a particular role. In the past couple of years at Leap Companies, we have hired a project coordinator, a project manager, and a business development manager. Previously, these three key roles were my responsibility. Now prospecting for new business, managing existing business, and dealing with day-to-day issues within a project are now broken up into three roles. When hiring for each of those positions, I had to determine the person's personality and coachability, along with their desire to learn the business. This took a lot of patience on my side, answering questions and spending one-on-one time together. Initially, this doubled my workload, but it was my job to coach and mentor the people I hired so they could become self-sufficient. Doing so creates company loyalty, and those three people are still with Leap Companies today. They are self-sufficient and know their roles and responsibilities. Certainly, we are in contact throughout the day, and it's interesting to see these people coming to me with suggestions for process improvement initiatives; they have more time to spend on improvements and pushing the business forward. This frees up more of my time, so this is truly a win-win for all of us, which benefits the business overall.

The one caution to keep in mind when deciding when to hire and for what roles is this: be sure that your business needs that particular role to be filled at a particular time because it benefits the business. Don't hire someone simply because it benefits you. I've made this mistake and have hired the wrong person at the wrong time. Even though I wanted to delegate the responsibilities for that role, I wasn't ready to do so, and the business wasn't financially ready. This particular role should have been a temporary position, and when the business got slow, I had to let the person go. In hindsight I had put time and energy into training this person, and I should have found ways to keep them busy. Letting this person go was like throwing money down the drain.

CHALLENGE YOUR OWN MINDSET

As an entrepreneur you are probably thinking, *Why do I need these additional roles? I've been doing this all long, and the business has to flow through me to be successful.*

My answer is simple. You can't spend all of your time focused on the day to day of your business. If you want your company to grow and expand, you need time to think, to envision, to be part of a business group. Because you can't see what is down the road if you're too busy only seeing what is directly in front of you. Certainly, at the outset, hiring someone is going to cost you time and your company money. But if you hire the right people at

If you want your company to grow and expand, you need time to think, to envision, to be part of a business group.

the right time, you and your company will benefit multiple times over.[33] I can personally tell you that if you are getting to a point that you're feeling overwhelmed and can't keep up with the demands of your business, if you're having sleepless nights and you're doing whatever it takes to keep your business going, including

working eighty-hour workweeks, then it's probably time to hire so that you can offload some of your responsibilities. You only have so much mental, emotional, and physical bandwidth, and your company could suffer a major calamity if you end up in the hospital.

Perhaps your business is five to ten years old. It's got some maturity, and you are beginning to think, "What else can I do to potentially grow or expand my business?"

The first answer to that question is another question: Can your business currently operate without your day-to-day involvement? That doesn't mean that you're not involved, but you have to make sure that your company can operate with no more than about 20 percent of your involvement.

---

33   To help you determine the right steps to take and when to take them, I recommend reading *Good to Great* by Jim Collins and *What Got You Here Won't Get You There* by Marshall Goldsmith.

Years ago I made a costly mistake with Leap. The business was going through a slow year of sales, so I thought I could take this time to establish and grow my recruiting business. However, the only thing I succeeded in doing was to double my time and energy commitments, and neither of my companies benefitted from me being pulled in two different directions. I made my life a lot more complicated by trying to run two businesses at the same time and making all the decisions. I was fortunate to hire Chris to take over the recruiting business so that I could refocus on the restaurant furnishing company.

A word to the wise: If you want to add another division, DBA, or a new business to your current company, someone has got to be in the driver's seat. The 80/20 rule applies; you need 80 percent of your time to run your new endeavor, leaving you only 20 percent to run your current business. This rule will help you decide if the new endeavor is the right move to make and if you need to hire someone to run it for you.

LEAVE WORK AT WORK

In today's virtual world, it is easy to have office mobility. You can establish your office at a local coffee shop or office building. You can have company meetings from your car or hold client meetings from your home office. The key word is "mobility," which affords you flexibility. The drawback to having unlimited mobility is that, as a business owner, it is easy to forget when to "leave work at work." You can take an employee call at 10:00 p.m. or 5:00 a.m. You can connect via Zoom with a customer while taking your significant other out to dinner (e.g., "This is really important, honey, and I'll only be a few minutes"). But what your partner hears is that they are not important. The truth is that your business can be like a baby and consume twenty-four hours of your time seven days a week. This creates a tremendous amount of stress for you and for those you have relationship with.

This might seem "old school," but there is a good reason to have a physical office space or a physical building that you go to and from. The reason is that it creates physical and mental separation between your business life and your personal life. I got caught up in a 24/7 business mindset in the early years of running Leap. But I made a point of not doing any type of work when I was with my kids or spending time with my wife. The only exceptions were emergencies, and these had to be true emergencies. Today I rarely check emails or phone messages outside of my working hours. And to be honest, this has made me a better person. I have been integral to my children instead of being an absentee father. Mitzi and I have a great marriage because she knows that our time together is my priority. Leaving work at work has also made me more productive while at work. I know that I have X number of hours to get done what needs to be done, so I better get to it.

Here's my advice: no matter where your office is, when you close the door for the day, keep it closed until the next business day. You don't want to hear the words, "You're not married to your business! You're married to me!"

I learned this the hard way. My temperament and personality create a "lean" in me to always be accessible. Early in my career, I really struggled to maintain a separation between business and personal time. For example, my family and I took a vacation to Disney World years ago, and I was always on my phone checking emails and messages, replying back, and calling whomever I needed to. I thought I was being a good guy; I had paid for the family vacation, and I was there in body with them. But I really wasn't engaged with my family. A couple of days into our vacation, the despondent looks on my kids' faces and Mitzi's "I've had enough!" looks made me realize what I *wasn't* doing and what I *should* be doing. From that point forward to today, I set out of office replies and say, "Hey, I'm on vacation. Can I call you back next week?" Sure, a couple of people might feel put out, but most will gain a level of respect for you.

If you find that it is imperative to work during a family vacation or other family time, I suggest doing so during limited hours. For instance, you might tell your family that you need to work a particular morning or evening. You can always get up early to start your day or stay up late after they have gone to bed, allowing you to join your family on their schedule. This will allow you to clear your mind and enjoy whatever family activity is planned. Over the years I have talked to many entrepreneurs who keep the same type of schedule, whether morning or evening, then they feel like they can be fully present during the rest of the day.

FAMILY COMMUNICATION

With Mitzi growing up in a business environment—and today owning her own company—I was fortunate to marry someone who completely understood the complexities of business and the involvement needed from the business owner. But not every business owner has this luxury. From the outset of starting your business, it is important that your family knows what you are doing and why you are doing it. That isn't an excuse to justify putting your business ahead of your family (e.g., "I'm doing this for you!"). It means that everyone needs to understand that being in business is not like being an employee of a company. If that was the type of life you wanted, you would have punched in and out at a factory. It is crucial that everyone you're in relationship with understands the commitment and sacrifice needed to start and grow a successful company. And it is imperative that you, as the owner, understand the commitment and sacrifice you need to make in order to meet your partner's needs and your family's needs.

TIME IS ON YOUR SIDE ... SORT OF

Years ago there was a song put out by the rock band the Rolling Stones called "Time Is on My Side." As a business owner, time is on your side ... sort of. Here's what I mean.

Your business needs you. That's a given. It needs your attention, and it needs your time. The best way to help your family understand this is to say something like, "If I worked for someone else, I would have to be at my job for the hours that job called for. Most likely, I wouldn't be available for phone calls, to check emails, etc. The time I spend at work on my business is similar. I can't commit to answering phone calls, emails, text messages, etc. when you want me to." So your time isn't your own.

Having said that, owning your own business gives you the ability to flex your time. Your daughter has a recital at school, your son is playing a team sport, your spouse or partner needs you to be at an appointment. For important times such as these, most of the time you can schedule your work around these important engagements. It really comes down to setting your priorities. So I challenge you: if work comes first and relationships second, what does that say about your priorities? Looking long term, you can build your business over ten, twenty, or thirty years, but what did you miss out on during those years?

Running our own businesses, Mitzi and I fully understand the need to balance work and relationships. At times it isn't easy. But running our businesses has given us the freedom to provide financially for our family while giving us the time flexibility we need. If my son is playing in a golf tournament, I'm there to support him. If Mitzi has to run out to the high school because my daughter needs something, she can do so. Conversely, my kids know that if either of us has to take a call in the evening, they don't feel slighted. To some extent everyone is inconvenienced in order to accommodate everyone's schedules and needs. In my view having this type of personal freedom and time flexibility is one of the great benefits of being a business owner, and it is definitely one of the main reasons I've chosen this lifestyle.

KEEPING YOUR HANDS OFF THE WHEEL

As you transition roles and responsibilities in your business to other people, it is natural to have fears, worries, or anxieties, no matter how competent these people are from the get-go. Will this salesperson treat customers the way I would? Will this CFO handle the company's finances the way I would? Would this secretary answer the phone the way I would? What is the common denominator in these questions and others like them? The word "I," meaning you, the business owner.

Expecting someone to handle their roles and responsibilities exactly the way you would is a misnomer. It simply isn't going to happen. Granted, you will train and impart to them according to the way your business runs. However, you hired these people as individuals, and they will bring their personalities, their experiences, their education, and much more to their jobs. You don't want individuals to be carbon copies of you; if that happened, your business wouldn't grow. It takes people who are outside of your box and your way of thinking to bring new ideas and fresh perspectives. So get used to feeling the anxiousness that comes with hiring someone new to do something you've been doing. However, don't let that person know you feel anxious; let them know that you have "every confidence" in their ability to fulfill their responsibilities. Do this from day one of hiring. And just because one person doesn't work out doesn't mean you shift back from imparting your confidence in the next hire to telling them why the other person didn't work about and you are afraid the new hire will make the same mistakes. If past mistakes are the barometer for your business, it would have failed long ago because of the mistakes that you have made!

LEAPING FORWARD ⊕

PAT'S POINTS TO PONDER

- If you want your business to grow past you, you have to decide when and how you can live with management and decisions that take place outside you.

- In order to begin to scale your business, it has to operate without you being the center of its universe.

- No matter if you're in the start-up phase or running a mature business, at some point you'll want to sell your company, so you should start with the "end in mind."

- Always remind yourself that you are reinvesting in your business for long-term gain. "Short-term pain for long-term gain."

- Be sure that your business needs that particular role to be filled at a particular time because it benefits the business.

- If you want to add another division, DBA, or a new business to your current company, someone has got to be in the driver's seat.

- Having personal freedom and time flexibility is one of the great benefits of being a business owner.

CHAPTER 16

Here Comes the Curveball!

When life throws you a curveball, don't let it knock you down and keep you down. Get up, readjust, brush yourself off and keep moving forward.

—GEORGE BRONNER

A s a baseball aficionado, I love statistics. Consider the following about the curveball, which is one of the hardest pitches to hit:[34]

A curveball is a breaking pitch that has more movement than just about any other pitch. It is thrown slower and with more overall break than a slider, and it is used to keep hitters off-balance. When executed correctly by a pitcher, a batter expecting a fastball will swing too early and over the top of the curveball.

The curveball has been one of the most commonly used pitches throughout baseball history, and the universally

---

34   MLB, "Curveball (CU)," accessed May 25, 2023, https://www.mlb.com/glossary/pitch-types/curveball.

accepted signal for a curveball is a catcher putting down two fingers.

The pitch is so well known in American culture that the phrase "throw a curveball" has emerged as an idiom. Like the goal of pitchers when throwing the pitch, the idiom "to throw a curve" means to trick someone with something unexpected.

In business—as in any area of life—you are sometimes thrown a curveball that not only didn't you see coming, but you were also never prepared for. And as in baseball, most often you "swing and miss." But with practice, seeing a curveball coming before it gets to you can help you make "contact."

You are sometimes thrown a curveball that not only didn't you see coming, but you were also never prepared for.

In early 2023 I was thrown a curveball that I never saw coming. So I thought it was important to close this book with what will happen to everyone at some point in their business. It's reality. Curveballs come at different shapes and sizes, and one will come your way, so you need to be ready to either hit it or let it pass you by.

My business partner, Chris, and I were trying to work out a deal where he would buy my shares of the recruiting business, a stand-alone company under the Leap Companies. Over the past eight years, he had earned 49 percent of the equity based on his productivity. I owned the remaining 51 percent, and I was ready to exit the business for many different reasons.

I had asked Chris to make me an offer of what he thought was fair. I did not set any price, and he came back with an offer I thought was equitable. I then told him I could finance the deal for five years, so we hired an attorney to draft the agreement. I thought, *This will be good for both of us*, and that's when the curveball came.

A couple weeks of weeks later, Chris called me to say he was struggling with the decision and had been offered a job to run a staffing company. He was unsure if this is something he should pursue versus buying the company. While on the surface that might sound legitimate, over the years Chris has said similar things to me based on the success the business was having, and I quickly realized this was a negotiation ploy. I sighed with disappointment. When he had finished talking, I said, "That's a real decision, if that's true. You do what's in the best interest of you and your family, but I've got to know by Monday because I can't keep going through this. We have gone down this business path, and now you're throwing a curveball. Take the weekend and talk to your wife, but you need to make a decision by Monday because I'm not going back and forth with you any longer."

On Monday morning Chris was the first one to call me. However, he did not bring up the staffing company job. Instead, he went right into what he wanted to offer for my recruiting company, which was *half* of what he originally offered—or what he said he was going to offer. I've always known that Chris could produce; he is a tremendous salesman. I was willing to bankroll him, but he blew this curveball right by me.

Just like in baseball, when a batter steps out of the batter's box to regroup, I did the same on this call with Chris. I took a few moments, then said, "I've got to reflect on this. I can't give you an answer yes or no, but we have two other options. The first is you buying me out, and me now agreeing to a last-minute offer that is way less than your original proposal. The second is that I can continue to run the recruiting business and hire someone to do your job … if you're truly unhappy here." Then a third option came into my mind, and I said, "I could also close down the recruiting company and let you go do what you want to go do." He had a noncompete, so I told him I was going to take a few days to reflect on our conversation.

A couple of hours after my call with Chris, for some strange reason, I got his calendar invites through my phone. And guess what. Another curveball came my way.

The calendar invite and email was from a good friend of Chris's and a guy whom we hired a couple of months prior. However, the email was not from my company's address but from "Leap Brands." This guy had created a new identity called Leap Brands and was using *our* company's email system to communicate with *our* clients and employees without my knowledge!

I was now starting to see a clear picture of what was happening in the recruiting company. Over the past couple of months, billings were way down, and I now knew why. So I took a picture of the calendar invite and email and sent it back to my new employee, with no comment from me. The next thing I knew, my phone is blowing up with text and voice mails: "It's not like you think it is." "It's not the way it seems." But I didn't respond.

I talked to Mitzi that night, and I also talked to some of my EO guys from my business group. I wanted to talk out my thoughts and get clarity. By the end of the evening, I knew I only had one card left to play: I would shut down the recruiting company. My decision had nothing to do with money and everything to do with trust. The easy decision would have been to accept Chris's alternative offer to buy me out. But I couldn't trust the fact that he would come with the money at closing. I also knew what my company had in the bank and what I could walk away with unscathed.

The next morning I called Chris and said, "I'm shutting down the recruiting company."

To his credit, he replied, "I can respect your decision."

After a couple of minutes, I wished him well, then hung up.

Over the next couple of weeks, I carried a lot of sadness inside of me. While I've never been divorced, in some ways I felt like I was going through a business "divorce." And I'm very thankful that I had Mitzi and my business group to help me work through my thoughts and feelings.

LESSONS LEARNED

In business sometimes you have to learn things the hard way by making mistakes and missing the "curveballs" that come your way. However, as business owner you can either wallow in self-pity and let that curveball knock you out of the batter's box, or you can take a little time to readjust and get back in the game again.

When I look back at my relationship with Chris, I can truly say that I wanted him to succeed, and I was willing to put in the time and effort needed. I was even going to give him the first right to purchase the Leap Companies as part of a long-term agreement. I thought a lot of him as a person, and I thought we were on the right path together.

As a business owner, you might have a "Chris" in your company. However, as business owners you and I can't have blind trust in people, whether they are our employees or customers. As I learned with Chris, a small amount of skepticism can be healthy.

When I look back over the past several years, had I been a little skeptical, I would have seen the "curveball" from Chris coming a long time ago. He never seemed content or happy with whatever I gave him. I wanted to groom him to become CEO, but while he was a heck of a sales guy, I failed to ask myself the question, "Can he lead?" Instead, I assumed he could, so I tried to control the path that would make him the CEO instead of letting objectivity and an analytical mindset guide me.

Perhaps you are considering hiring someone to lead a department or division within your company. Maybe you are making your first hiring decision for your start-up company. In either case it is important to consider the skill set this person brings to the table. But it's just as important to truly know who this person is. What makes them tick inside? What is their character truly like? To what degree can they be trusted, and with what can they be trusted?

As I look back on Chris's time with my company, he was always about moving up the ladder and wanting a different title. Now ambition is a great trait, so don't get me wrong. But impatient ambition is a red flag. I would caution you with the following:

- Be aware when someone is never satisfied.

- Be alert to any drama points in relationships that are not valid.

- Be leery of someone who makes quick decisions without understanding the consequences.

- Be cautious when someone is always wanting to negotiate or renegotiate.

When Chris told me on the phone that he wanted to offer me less than half of his original offer, he never thought through the consequences of "If I take this action, what are Pat's options?"

I fully understand that in business, there are times when a decision must be made on the spur of the moment. But most decisions are not life or death, and as the owner you can think through any decision before you. It's also important to surround yourself with people who can take a step back and think through with you what is about to happen.

With Chris, I should have better understood that he was impulsive. I was the no guy a lot because I saw the consequences for different decisions. I think that frustrated him, and I should have been a better leader in communicating, saying something like, "I know there are things that you want to do. But you need to trust me as someone with a lot of experience. You have the gift to sell, but you also have a blind spot in that you don't see the consequences. My gift is to see the big picture, the overall vision from a ten thousand view." But because I didn't clearly communicate what I knew to be true, Chris thought I was simply a naysayer, and he started to devalue what I brought to the table.

As a business owner, whether it's an employee or a customer, if someone begins to downplay your role, I advise you to take a step back and try to figure out what's really going on. Some people might be risk-takers, and they might interpret your cautionary ways as holding them back. Other people might have a hidden agenda that motivates them. If the latter is the case, that agenda will eventually surface. So don't dismiss your gut instinct if you sense something isn't right but can't put your finger on it.

As I wanted to do with Chris, you may want to be a mentor to someone in your business. You want to set that person up for success. But always ask yourself, "Is this person ready to handle the success that can come their way?" Do they have the maturity, or could success go to their head and turn them into someone you are not looking for them to be?

To state the obvious, people have different temperaments and personalities, and they bring their own perspectives, their own "learned lens" to the table. And that's what makes the business world go round and round. You will never see eye to eye 100 percent, and allowing for different perspectives will help you maintain an objective mindset. But if there is constant friction in the path you are walking with an employee or customer, you have to ask yourself what is really going one. Otherwise, you'll never see the curveball that's coming your way.

VALUES

I talked about the importance of values earlier in this book, but the significance of having the same core values cannot be overstated. What happened with Chris was the reason why I decided to take an honest look at my own core values and why I took the time with my employees to establish our company's core values. As a business owner, your company needs to reflect who you are and how you do business, and your hiring practices should be aligned to those core values. When it comes time for employee reviews, you should include a time of making sure their values are aligned with the company's. Core values are a fundamental element on how you can grow a business. They are also how you hold your employees—and even customers—accountable to your business practices.

In my recruiting business, I lost sight of my and my company's core values. That was part of the reason things went array with Chris. I'm not saying whose core values were right or wrong, but I am saying we were not aligned, and I didn't realize that soon enough.

MOVING ON

The old saying "You can't cry over spilled milk" is apropos for business. When a situation goes sideways, you can't have a woe-is-me mindset, or you'll never move on. It's important to understand what happened and why it happened so that you don't repeat the same mistake. But don't let mistakes derail you. Mistakes are the stepping stones to finding the right path that leads to success.

When I made the decision to dissolve my recruiting company, I knew that the Leap Companies would take a big hit. It would have been easy to bemoan the loss of that revenue, but I needed to look at how prosperous the company was for the past ten years, and I now had the opportunity to look at other options. As my mother-in-law is noted for saying to her family, "Don't look back." Instead, you've got to say, "What's next? Where are we going?"

For my business, I've decided to move forward and create a web-based store to sell our products online, which will complement our project-based furniture business. It's a big move, and I'm creating a bigger brand, where my company can use our collective knowledge and all the products that we have and sell direct to the consumer, to the small independent restaurant, to a chef expanding his patio so we can reach a new type of customer.

Regarding my recruiting business, instead of saying, "Why in the world did I do that?" I remind them and myself that we did well, we learned a lot, and we had fun growing a profitable business. But as the saying goes, all good things come to an end at some point.

Closing the recruiting business has pushed me into developing other new business opportunities and has created a new excitement for my company and me. We are back in the growth element, and I couldn't be happier!

I'd like to wrap up this chapter by saying that business is lived in real time. And life is lived in real time. But both business and life can't be lived looking in the rearview mirror. You've got to keep moving forward if you want to succeed.

PAT'S POINTS TO PONDER

- Curveballs come at different shapes and sizes, and one will come your way, so you need to be ready to either hit it or let it pass you by.

- If a curveball gets by you, step outside of the "batter's box" and regroup, then get back to business.

- When you're considering someone for a management position, take a good look at their skill set, then ask yourself, "Can this person lead?"

- There are times when you need to make a snap decision, but most are not life or death. Take time to think through what you are going to do, and when possible, talk to someone who can be a sounding board.

TAKE THE LEAP

Whether you are just starting out or have a viable business, as an entrepreneur you are following your own path—a path you were meant to travel. But that path will zig and zag. It will run into dead ends and lead to wide open possibilities. However, if you don't keep following your path to wherever it leads you, you will always feel that something is missing in your life. So I encourage you to keep moving forward; keep fighting the fight because part of your success is simply showing up every day.

As we part ways, I'm going to leave you with some final points.

- Having walked the entrepreneurial path for more than sixteen years, I can tell you that every emotion known to humanity will come up at some point. But you can't let emotions rule your decisions. You have to think through what you want to do and, to the best of your ability, determine potential outcomes. No matter the outcome, doing this will help you manage your expectations so you don't get too high or too low. You also have to own your decisions because you will be the one who reaps the rewards and learns from the consequences.

- No matter what happens on a daily basis, never let your emotions take control of your business or get the better of you. There's nothing wrong with being emotional, but emotions can cloud your judgment. So take a step back and a deep breath when your emotions are starting to direct your business decisions. Over the past sixteen years, if I had allowed my emotions to affect my decisions, I can tell you with certainty that I would not be in business today. But I had to constantly reminded myself of my desire to have personal freedom because I didn't want to work for someone else and of the financial freedom I wanted to attain. With that in mind, during the hard times, I simply had to figure out what would work in that moment and be ready to pivot, to adapt, and to not be rigid in my thinking.

- You also have to be able to pivot in the moment and make adjustments and transitions as needed. So you can't keep doing things the way you've been doing them because "that's the way they've always been done." Adaptation and following your instincts are keys to business success.

- As an entrepreneur you desire personal and financial freedom that working for someone else will never bring you. And when the inevitable hard times come, remind yourself that you are embracing the freedom to follow your path—and keep going. Giving up is only an option when every door is closed and every opportunity has been exhausted. So don't give up too soon; you might only be twenty-four hours from the breakthrough you've been waiting for.

- In my years in business, I've heard the words "just give up" many times in my head. However, I never had a plan B in place, so giving up has never been an option. Had I done so, I wouldn't have the lifestyle and the freedom to live life on my own terms that I have today. Yes, business is a grind. An everyday grind. But that's what we sign up for as entrepreneurs.

- When you're first starting out, understand that the business world is not a "bed of roses." If you have already established your company, you know how true that statement is. You have to be ready for the unexpected, good and bad, and be nimble and flexible in your business *and* your thought process. While you want to take your company in a specific direction, when the opportunity to take a "right or left turn" comes up—one that will make you some extra cash—you have to take this into serious consideration. Just I did, you need to have the foresight to walk through a door and take a path that you don't know where it will end. Doing so will help you define and refine your business and your niche.

- You have to have a vision for your business and for your personal life. Unless you have a vision, you'll always be chasing the "wind" with no direction and no purpose. While that vision needs to be stable, it also needs to be flexible. That's what happened to Leap Companies when I decided to change from a food distributor for ice and margarita machines to furniture and recruiting.

Having a vision for your business keeps you on track and also allows you to open the door when opportunity comes knocking.

That's exactly what happened in my initial meetings with the Cordish Companies. I saw this very large company that needed a lot of help, and I went through that door—even though I had no idea what I was doing at the time! However, once we decided to do business together, that was the start of literally building my company, and seeing my vision of running a successful company come to pass.

The vision I had for my life and business and the passion to achieve that vision kept me moving forward during the tough times and allowed me to "enjoy the moment" in the good times. It was this type of thinking that led me to change Leap Companies from a floundering food equipment distributor for ice and margarita machines into successful restaurant furniture and recruiting business.

In closing I challenge you to ask yourself, "What vision do I have for my life and business? How do these visions dovetail together? How can I be flexible, nimble, adaptable, and pivot when necessary in order to keep my personal and business visions fresh and alive?" Your answers will be the driving force to keep you moving forward. As your fellow entrepreneur, I encourage you to keep fighting the good fight!

PAT'S BASIC BUSINESS RULES

1. It is what it is.

2. Control what you can control.

3. Bird in the hand early on. Two in the bush when you can risk it, or when the bird keeps pooping in your nest, or you have too many birds.

4. Family is good to come home to, not to partner with in business.

5. Listen to your spouse! They typically have more common sense than you, even if you don't want to admit it.

6. Don't poke the bear. Feed him so he becomes your friend over time.

7. Take the bullet. It won't kill you; it will actually make you stronger.

8. Show up + follow through = success.

9. Plan on no plans working out the way you thought they would.

10. Be Gumby while you build.

11. There is no brand until you show you are a brand.

12. Exercise. It's the only thing that will keep you sane.

BONUS FOR A BAKER'S DOZEN!

13. Long term only lasts so long. Pay yourself first.

ABOUT THE AUTHOR

P at Phelan is the founder and CEO of the Leap Companies and an entrepreneur, visionary, and strategic thinker in the world of hospitality. He has raised more than $100 million in private equity for various hospitality projects, supplied and manufactured more than $75 million in hospitality furniture, and recruited hundreds of talented people for some of the top food and beverage brands. Pat received his bachelor's in business from the University of Missouri-Columbia and his MBA from Keller Graduate School of Management. Pat was named as one of the Nation's Restaurant News 2018 top 75 power CEOs in hospitality. Leap was named one of Kansas City's top 100 growing companies in 2018, 2019, and 2020 by *Ingram's* magazine.

Pat resides in Kansas City, Missouri, with his wife, Mitzi, and their two beautiful daughters, Jenna and Jamie.

ABOUT LEAP COMPANIES

The Leap Companies, founded in 2006 and headquartered in Kansas City, Missouri, has two primary divisions: Leap Hospitality and Leap Strategic. Leap Hospitality focuses on manufacturing and distributing furniture and case goods to the hospitality industry. Leap Strategic focuses on executive search and mergers and acquisitions with multistate service, retail and hospitality companies, private equity firms, and family offices.

LEAP'S VISION/MISSION

Each team member, vendor, client, or candidate has their own personal journey. Whether it's scaling your concept, promoting your ideas, fulfilling a new career, or building out your company's team, Leap Companies's mission is to help you fulfill that journey in a meaningful, positive way.

Printed in the USA
CPSIA information can be obtained
at www.ICGtesting.com
JSHW021256171023
50337JS00002B/57